SEEING IT THROUGH
HALIFAX & CALDERDALE
DURING WORLD WAR II

Published by Peter Thomas
Woodleigh, Savile Road,
Hebden Bridge, West Yorkshire

Printed in Great Britain by
Pennine Printing Services
Ripponden, West Yorkshire, England
A Member of Jarvis Print Group
Manchester, England

ISBN 0 9535405 2 9

Front Cover: Air raid drill in 1939 for girls of Holy Trinity Senior School.
Back Cover: Local Home Guard Heraldry.

Seeing It Through - Halifax & Calderdale During World War II

The author is aware that the local government area of Calderdale did not exist until the 1970s.
The term has been used as a convenient shorthand as it perfectly covers the geographical scope of this book.

By Peter Thomas

ACKNOWLEDGEMENTS

Special thanks are due to the following: -

Frank Woolrych, who has been typically generous with his time and expertise on the images, some of which came from the Alice Longstaff Collection.

Issy Shannon, who has been equally generous with advice, encouragement and loan of materials.

Scott Flaving at Wellesley Barracks for access to the Home Guard file.

Calderdale MBC for permission to reproduce photographs and other archival evidence.

The help of Pauline Lancaster, at the Reference section of the Halifax Central Library and John Spencer, at Bankfield Museum, has been particularly appreciated.

Stephen Gee, who has freely allowed access to his astonishing photograph collection.

The trustees of the Birchcliffe Heritage Centre – Oral History Archives.

Local newspapers have been of great assistance in providing information, in particular, the 'Halifax Evening Courier.' Articles concerning the Hanson Lane bomb (Veronica O'Brien), the Halifax and Elland Spitfire Funds (Edward Riley), and the Channel Island evacuees (Virginia Mason), have been particularly helpful.

A full list of all who contributed towards this book in terms of providing information and/or photographs can be found at the back. Both letters and interviews were a rich source of personal anecdotes, although, sadly, some of the contributors are no longer with us.

Last, but not least, a heartfelt thanks to my wife, Louise, for word-processing and providing support in innumerable ways.

CONTENTS

SEEING IT THROUGH –
HALIFAX AND CALDERDALE DURING WORLD WAR II

INTRODUCTION

Mine was the generation that just 'missed' the war. Having been born in 1941, for me only the vaguest of memories linger – of soldiers billeted in the local church hall; of a huge parade along Market Street, Hebden Bridge, probably part of a 1945 'Victory in Europe' celebration. Young as I was, however, the phrase, "Got any gum chum?" had entered my consciousness, one of the many by-products of the massive American presence in the country. We relentlessly bombarded the soldiers with this request whenever they moved in and out of the church hall, but good humoured as they were, I doubt that chewing gum or any other sort of confectionery was forthcoming from their meagre British soldier rations. Nevertheless, cadging did bring a reward much greater than gum – a tin mug which proved to be a valuable asset to my family as shortages of all kinds continued for years to come.

As the war ended, my generation moved on into school, serene and secure under a benign government suffused with the idealism of the Welfare State. Austerity and rationing continued, not ending completely until 1954, but we enjoyed free milk and subsidised dinners, blissfully unaware of how different it might all have been, of how close we had come to the shadow of tyranny.

And how could we have known? We knew of classmates who had suffered personal family loss, but throughout my time at school, we were taught nothing of World War Two, a titanic struggle for freedom, which cost the lives of 55 million people. The history syllabus seemed to peter out with the 19th Century Factory Acts, and the war was pushed quietly aside. Perhaps it was considered 'unBritish' to dwell on such matters, but we were left to make what we

could of it out of comics and films – a war reduced to hapless and witless 'Huns' or 'Japs' falling in heaps before the withering fire of the heroic Allies. It was much later that I began to realise the scale of the sacrifice involved in defeating fascism and what a close run thing it had been.

Plenty has now been written of such matters, as World War Two has become an essential component of the media industry. As for this book, its focus is on the people of Halifax and district during those epic years of 1939 to 1945. It is about life on the Home Front and the generation that had to 'see it through.' Halifax never had to suffer the ordeal of a prolonged bombing 'blitz' in the fashion of nearby cities such as Manchester and Sheffield. The dramas of 'dogfights' between Spitfires and Messerschmitts belonged more to the skies above Kent than to those above Halifax.

To say, however, that "nothing happened" in this area is very far from the truth. The Second World War was fought on such an immense scale that it involved everyone. Halifax and Calderdale became

---

"Halifax and Calderdale became just one cog in a huge, national fighting machine"

---

just one cog in a huge, national fighting machine and 'total' war demanded that civilians should play their part to the hilt. Many local factories were pressed directly into the war effort, and with so many men conscripted into the armed forces, the pressure was on women to replace them on the factory floor. Some women chose to join the drive to produce more food, finding in the Land Army a mixture of drudgery and exhilarating freedom.

As if long hours in factories or on the land were not enough, civilians were expected and sometimes compelled to make an extra effort in their 'free time' by engaging in fire-watching or joining such organisations as the Auxiliary Fire and Ambulance Services, Air Raid Precaution or the Home Guard. They were also cajoled into contributing truly amazing sums of money into a succession of war savings drives. Halifax also became part of that strange wartime phenomenon of a nation seemingly on the move. As local men donned uniform and left, other men in uniform arrived to replace them. The area became filled with strangers billeted in factories and church halls. More strangers arrived in the shape of evacuees, mainly children – successive waves in 1939, 1940 and 1944. Again the sensation was of movement, constant ebb and flow. The soldiers were often 'in transit;' the evacuees often returned home as soon as it was deemed safe to do so.

So much for the view that "nothing happened" around here during the war. Everyone's life was affected to a lesser or greater degree on a scale that ranged from the hardships of rationing and shortages to the tragedy of the loss of one or more loved ones. Yet it was not all negative. Because of the war, enduring friendships were forged between people who would otherwise never have met, and this applied particularly to the evacuees. Again, those who lived through those momentous years often reflect fondly on the unity and purpose that was felt throughout the nation at large, a feeling of togetherness in the fighting of a just war. Memories of those times are often clearly etched in the mind, showing that if all life is a drama of one sort or another, then a wartime backdrop of fear, uncertainty and hope gives a sharper edge to it all. Amidst these sometimes conflicting feelings the people of Halifax and the surrounding district simply had to get their heads down, keep their spirits up and 'see it through.' This book is dedicated to the generation that did just that.

THAT FATEFUL BROADCAST

"I have to tell you now that no such undertaking has been received, and that consequently this country is at war with Germany."
Neville Chamberlain,
Sunday September 3rd 1939.

Just as 24 years later, everyone remembered just where they were and what they were doing when they heard the news of the assassination of President J.F. Kennedy, the same applies to that balmy September morning when the British Prime Minister came on the radio at 11.15 am to announce the news that Hitler had ignored that British ultimatum to evacuate Poland. Everyone must have known that a significant moment in history had arrived, but nobody knew the precise long-term significance for his or her own life and, predictably, responses varied.

Marjorie Talbot of Claremount, Halifax, immediately burst into tears. Her boyfriend, Jim Brennan, was a regular soldier, a bandsman in the Black Watch. She knew that he would be sent immediately to France, but…what then? In

Jim Brennan….bound for France.

Marjorie Talbot….deep anxiety.

total contrast, Mary Prout of Halifax greeted Chamberlain's broadcast with delight. On holiday with friends in the Isle of Man, she fondly imagined that the outbreak of war would not allow her to return home. She would be 'condemned' to a holiday 'for the duration.' Alas, the illusion was soon to be shattered!

Ten year old Stanley Topliss of Lees Road, Hebden Bridge, spent the afternoon of September 3rd filling tin cans full of water, assisted by his young friend, Tom Southwell. This was in preparation for an incendiary attack, and with that curious logic of children, both he and Tom became convinced that the Germans never bombed Hebden Bridge because Hitler knew about the tin cans. Across in Elland, Lewis Robertshaw was in the act of putting a penny in the cap of a tramp, who was playing a fiddle in the street, when his mother called him in to hear the news. The tramp was a World War One veteran, and so in this one moment Lewis had established a strange connection between a fading past and an ominous future.

If that warm September morning had a touch of Indian summer about it, for John and Nellie Wall of Spring Hall Lane, Halifax, the day was to contain nothing but the dark clouds of anxiety. Their 6 year old daughter, June, had a hole in her heart, a condition which was inoperable in those days. At the very limit, she was not expected to live beyond the age of 15. John, aged 33, was a clerk at the engineering firm of Hattersley's, and for the time being this was a reserved occupation, saving him from conscription. However, how long would this last? Every moment spent with a dying daughter was precious to him, but there was a real prospect that a call-up might come, and that the parting with June might be a final one. Chamberlain's broadcast heralded a time of uncertainty for everyone, but for some the moment held more poignancy than for others.

June Wall....a hole in the heart.

It was not as if, however, the onset of war came as a 'bolt from the blue.' Although Neville Chamberlain seemed to have averted war by means of the infamous Munich Agreement in September 1938, when Hitler broke the agreement by taking over the whole of Czechoslovakia in March 1939, the coming of war seemed to be only a matter of time.

In terms of the defence of Britain's civilian population, the government's focus was on the threat from enemy bomber aircraft. Many thousands of British cinemagoers had watched in horrified silence as the newsreels from the Spanish Civil War had shown the destructive onslaught from the air on the Spanish Basque town of Guernica. The havoc had been wrought by German bombers, and presumably the same could be done to British cities. The pessimistic forecast in 1932, of the future British Prime Minister Stanley Baldwin, had been: "The bomber will always get through." It was not simply high explosive and incendiary bombs that were feared. The British government harboured a particular horror of the prospect of a mass gas attack from the air, and so hoping for the best but fearing the worst, the government set about preparing the country's defences. Perhaps the more difficult task, however, was to convince people of the reality of the threat.

The first mention of air raid precaution in government literature comes surprisingly early. In July 1935 a circular was sent to local authorities urging them to make plans. More forcibly, the Air Raid Precaution Act of 1937 required local authorities to submit their plans for government scrutiny. At a local level this was not yet taken seriously, although by 1937 a Halifax Air Raid Precaution Committee was in existence and offering safety advice. Evidence of some local concern was demonstrated when, in January 1938, Colonel W. Garforth from the Home Office Air Raid Precaution Department addressed a crowded meeting in Halifax. The concern over the use of gas was highlighted when Stoney Royd at Halifax was selected as an anti-gas training centre in March 1938. The following month, members of the Halifax Round Table volunteered for Air Raid

John Wall with daughter June....in happier days.

Precaution work, or ARP as it had now become widely known.

The September 1938 crisis over Czechoslovakia issued a 'hurry up' call. "Peace for our time," proclaimed the Prime Minister to cheering Downing Street crowds after the

---

"Huge casualties were expected in the event of an air attack"

Munich Agreement. The feeling of relief, however, was tempered in some by a new found sense of reality. Harold Doyle of Halifax was already engaged in war work at the engineering firm of Asquith's. He felt even then that time had only been bought; that the next crisis would be 'it;' and that British people should now be prepared to stand up to Hitler. The new mood of urgency was galvanising the government. Huge casualties were expected in

the event of an air attack, and in November 1938 an outstanding administrator was put in charge of ARP – Sir John Anderson. Expenditure on ARP quickly rose from £9.5 million to £51 million per year. A mass evacuation of all schoolchildren and mothers with children under 5 from danger areas to reception areas was planned. Thirty-eight million gas masks had already been distributed.

The new mood was certainly felt in Halifax and district. Volunteers dug trenches at places such as Savile Park in Halifax and Crow Wood Park in Sowerby Bridge. Above all, however, the fear of gas predominated. A consignment of 40,000 gas masks in need of assembly was dealt with by workers at the Paton and Baldwin and John Mackintosh factories, both of Halifax, who were taken off their normal assembly lines to deal with the work. At Elland the same feverish activity was undertaken by men, women and young people from the town's grammar school. The gas masks were fitted and distributed at various depots by volunteers from the ARP and the Women's Voluntary Service, or WVS, which immediately began to show its worth. In June 1938 Lady Reading had appealed for the establishment of a WVS for civil defence and many women had come forward. In self-mockery a volunteer later stated that WVS stood for 'Widows, Virgins and Spinsters,' but the organisation did sterling work throughout the war.

The arrival of gas masks in Halifax and Calderdale caused mixed feelings. On the one hand there was an eagerness to acquire them. At Akroyd Place, for example, 500 were fitted in less than four hours, but by 9 pm such large queues still remained that more than 100 people had to be turned away and dealt with the following day. On the other hand there was some revulsion at the sight of little children wearing gas masks. This was perhaps felt most keenly at the sight of the baby's version, the so-called 'helmet.' This could be likened to a transparent baby sized container with an airtight lid. At the head was a circular filter and, once the baby was inside, a pump attached to the side had to be operated constantly. One local mother was later to recollect that as she

Gas mask fitting session organised by the WVS

was in the process of doing a 'dummy run,' with baby ensconced inside, the child's grandmother entered the room. She immediately burst into tears. Her emotion can easily be understood – a tiny baby having to be protected from gas bombs falling at random from the sky. Had twentieth century civilisation come to this?

Fiction or horrific fact, the worst had to be prepared for. The government was, in secret, having hundreds of thousands of coffins made. On February 1st 1939, Halifax Town Council passed a £23,000 ARP scheme which included shelters and an underground first-aid post at Woolshops. As a reminder that there was business to be done further afield, a big recruiting rally was held in May 1939 in Halifax on behalf of the Duke of Wellington's Regiment, the famous local 'Dukes.' In June 1,200 young militiamen registered locally under the Compulsory Military Service Bill. The first ARP demonstration of how to react to an emergency was held at Queensbury in June, and in July 1939 a house was demolished on Grove Street, Halifax, as part of a big ARP

exercise. This was very much an occasion for ARP workers rather than the general public and included the clearing of debris, the treating of 'casualties,' gas decontamination, the use of a stirrup pump and a demonstration by the Auxiliary Fire Service. The fact that the house was very resistant to a quick demolition, may or may not have been encouraging.

It is very likely that there was little in the way of holiday mood during the summer of 1939. There was a weight of fearful expectancy in the air as Hitler built up the pressure on Poland, and on August 24th many thousands of schoolteachers were recalled early from their holidays to prepare for the evacuation of children from the cities. To some, everything had an air of unreality about it. The sandbagged buildings, the gas masks, the air raid shelters in process of being hastily erected – all seemed part of a bad dream. At the time of Munich in September 1938, Chamberlain had described similar scenes as "fantastic" and "incredible," the very words that now pinpointed the emotions of some people. Chamberlain had also wondered why British citizens should be

'The long and the short and the tall,' local recruits 1939.

Courtesy of Calderdale MBC Libraries, Museums and Arts.

toiling over such tasks because of a quarrel in a distant part of Europe, "between people of whom we know nothing." Wasn't Poland at least as far away as Czechoslovakia? Did we know any more of the Poles than we had of the Czechs? War had been averted once at the last minute – couldn't it be so again? Such 'clutching at straws' ended abruptly with that famous broadcast of Sunday, September 3rd 1939. Chamberlain's decision now to stand fast accorded with the wishes of the majority, even though Britain had not the slightest military capability of defending Poland at this moment. Shortly after the broadcast there was a widespread testing of air raid sirens across the country, including Halifax and Calderdale, triggering off alarm and, in some cases, panic. The question was…what next?

COUNTY BOROUGH OF HALIFAX.

AIR RAID PRECAUTIONS DEMONSTRATION
July 17th, 1939.

A Demonstration of certain A.R.P. Services will be held at—

SCOTT'S ROW, GROVE STREET,

(off NORTHGATE)

HALIFAX,

on Monday, July 17th, 1939, commencing 7-45 p.m.

PROGRAMME.

(a) Demolition of House with strengthened basement.

(b) Rescue Party at work clearing debris.

(c) First Aid Party dealing with casualties.

(d) Explosion of "Z" mixture Bomb to represent Gas Bomb.

(e) Decontamination Squad dealing with contaminated area.

(f) Incendiary Bombs—

    (i) In the open, burning powers of a Thermite Bomb—penetrating 22 gauge steel sheet, 1 foot of water and a sheet-metal water container.

    (ii) In the Hut, Electron Bomb to be extinguished by use of stirrup pump with dual nozzle spraying water.

(g) Auxiliary Fire Service—demonstrate the action of a Heavy Pump with crew in dealing with a fire in a house (smoke bombs used).

ALL A.R.P. workers are invited to attend and to wear the A.R.P. Badge when entering from Foundry Street.

Getting ARP prepared for the worst.

Courtesy of Calderdale MBC Libraries, Museums and Arts.

"WOT NO BOMBS?"

The lugubrious cartoon face of Chad peering over a wall and commenting on this or that shortage became a familiar one during the war. The comment usually referred to food but it might just as well have referred to enemy bombing for the first year of the war. Some bombs did fall in this period, which soon became labelled the 'phoney war,' but nothing like the terrific onslaught which had been feared and expected. In common with the rest of the country, Halifax had its Air Raid Precaution System prepared and ready to swing into action. The Halifax ARP Controller was the Town Clerk, Mr William Usher, and under the ARP Officer, Mr L. Massey, 1,500 volunteers had trained as part-time air raid wardens, ambulance drivers, auxiliary firemen/women and first aid workers. With regard to the last named, first-aid posts had been set up at numerous places; the one at Woodside Baths, Boothtown, contained a gas decontamination area with zinc partitions and showers. In October 1939 Halifax ran its biggest ARP exercise so far, but as the months passed with Halifax and Calderdale simply watching and waiting, it became a case of, "Wot no bombs?"

Nevertheless there was ample evidence that the war had begun. Shocking news from overseas demonstrated that civilians would very much be in the front line. The liner 'Athenia,' bound for Canada, had been torpedoed in the Atlantic by a German 'U'-boat virtually in the first hours of the war. Fortunately, Halifax citizens Mrs E.A. Moore and her daughter, Dorothy, were saved, along with Mr R.C. Barnes, who had been on his way to take up a teaching post in Ontario. Not so fortunate was Stoker Harry Haigh of Ploughcroft. He became the first local war casualty when he was drowned after the torpedoing of the aircraft carrier 'HMS Courageous,' in the Atlantic on September 18th 1939.

Nearer to home many local people were to feel the effects of the National Service (Armed Forces) Act of September 4th 1939, which made all males aged between 18 and 41 liable for conscription. If this was all a matter of due process, in contrast the effect of the outbreak of war on regular soldiers could be likened to a starting gun going off. One local woman had become engaged to a regular in the Green Howards just prior to the outbreak, anticipating a short leave if the worst came to the worst during which they could be married by special licence. However, once it all began, her fiancé's embarkation orders for India were so instant that he had to resort to throwing a letter to her out of the train window, requesting the finder to post it on. This was duly done, but the wedding was 'slightly' postponed – until November 1945, which was the next time they saw each other!

At the other end of the spectrum from those who went off instantly to fight were those who were not prepared to fight at all. If Britain was largely at one in its determination now to resist Hitler by force, it was not entirely so. The prospective conflict caused a good deal of heart-searching from a variety of viewpoints. The Communist 'Daily Worker' had initially supported the war as part of an anti-fascist crusade but, under orders from Moscow, it abruptly changed its stance shortly afterwards, now denouncing the conflict as a "capitalist war." This now caused many to part company with the extreme left, but some still opposed the war on grounds of religion or conscience or both. A prominent Hebden Bridge trades

Sowerby Bridge lads off to war.

Courtesy of Stephen Gee.

unionist of the time saw all this from the inside. As an engineer at Pickles` Foundry he observed the sudden 'about face' of the Communist sympathising shop-steward, and as a member of the Labour Party's League of Youth, he saw the agonising of friends torn between pacifism and a loathing of all that Hitler stood for.

This struggle of conscience was played out at a national level and during the war around 58,000 men and 2,000 women applied for registration as conscientious objectors. Conscience in this respect had to be proved and on October 24th 1939 the first Halifax conscientious objector appeared before a Leeds tribunal. Insufficient proof could lead to prosecution, and in the first case of its kind in the country a Halifax man, Frank Mitchell, was fined £1 in 1940 for failing to register for military service without proper reason. Conscription would be extended to unmarried women between the ages of 18 and 30 in December 1941, with a choice of joining the women's services, a civil defence organisation or entering industry. This led in 1942 to the appearance before a tribunal of Halifax's first female conscientious objector, Mary Holroyd, a 20 year old Jehovah's Witness.

Conscientious objectors were never popular, but there does not seem to have been the hatred directed at them that was such a feature of World War One. In fact, one Hebden Bridge business couple even hid a 'CO' on the run and found him a job. The long arm of the law eventually reached out and placed him in Armley Prison, but the couple continued their moral support by regularly visiting him.

The commencement of the war in Halifax and Calderdale was a serious enough event whatever one's political or moral views about it, and at first it seemed as if there was to be no light relief to soften the sombre days ahead. Halifax Town's fixture with Barrow was cancelled and the area's cinemas and theatres were closed. Fortunately these restrictions were very short-lived. Places of entertainment were soon reopened and wartime regional football leagues were set up. The young, with their eternal optimism, soon found a bright side to the war. Imagine the joy of pupils at elementary schools when they discovered that their return to school after the summer holidays was to be delayed for a week. Elementary schools in those days included pupils up to the school leaving age of 14 who had not left at 11 to attend grammar school, and so a large number of pupils were affected. Colin Wakefield, living at Lee Mount at this time, was one of these and his enforced absence from school lasted much longer than one week.

The problem facing the local authority was a lack of air raid shelters at schools and until these were hastily put in place, the risk could not be taken of having pupils on the premises. Happily or otherwise for Colin, the vicar of Lee Mount opened his church doors and offered a little teaching there. Philip Hanson was able to confirm that Colin's case was not an isolated one. As a pupil at Christ Church School, Pellon, Philip did return after the summer holidays of 1939, but the school was then closed for around six weeks for air raid shelters to be built. They were still not fully prepared even then and practices were held in the vicarage cellars. Another aspect of schooldays during the war, which impressed itself on Philip's mind, was the rapid turnover of teachers and the reappearance of older ladies who had clearly emerged from retirement to plug the gaps.

In these early weeks of the war, if it was the excitement of a change in routine that most impinged upon the young, the innovation which had the most drastic impact across the generations was the imposition of the blackout. If enemy bombers were to attack under cover of darkness, then it was to be made as difficult as possible for them to find their targets. From sunset on September 1st 1939, the day of Hitler's assault on Poland, throughout Britain no light had to show from windows; lights either stayed off or were heavily shaded; car headlights and rear lights had to be masked. "Put that light out," became one of the great catchphrases of the war as air raid wardens kept vigilant patrol through the streets at night. It fell upon householders to make their homes lightproof, having already in some cases criss-crossed their windows with sticky brown paper strips to try and limit damage from flying glass

Air raid drill at Holy Trinity School – smiling faces but a fearful prospect.
Courtesy of Calderdale MBC Libraries, Museums and Arts.

in the event of bombing. Help was at hand. Shops such as Baxter and Granger of Market Street, Halifax, advertised 'Lightproof Black Italian' at two shillings and sixpence (12.5p) per yard, or 'Lightproof Bolton Sheeting' at three shillings and eleven pence (20p). A cheaper alternative to material for curtains or blinds was to be found at Boots, where rolls of blackout paper were flying off the shelves at one shilling and sixpence (7.5p) per yard.

Having got the windows suitably blacked out, and the house darkened, the next problem was entry and exit without sending a flash of light through the doorway – the sort of thing to make an air raid warden bristle. In this respect much ingenuity was shown by members of Colin Wakefield's family at Lee Mount who rigged up a device by which, when the door was opened, a string attached to the handle operated a tube which slid neatly over the light bulb. This was proof that necessity really is the 'mother of invention,' and the device was much admired and copied by the Wakefields' neighbours. However, as always with DIY, some are more adept than others, and this can lead to unfortunate consequences. On September 20th 1939, a Halifax man died of gas poisoning from a punctured gas pipe, the result of tacking up blackout paper, one of the more bizarre accidents arising from the blackout.

The accidents, however, were mainly taking place on the streets. Within two weeks from September 1st 1939, road deaths doubled across the country (reaching over 4,000 by the end of 1939) and non-fatal accidents increased five-fold. The reasons for this carnage were simple. At best the streetlights were so heavily shaded as to give only the merest glimmer of light. Pedestrians were allowed to use a small torch which emitted a 'pencil' of light, and even then it could only be directed downwards. Around these virtually pitch-black streets cars rumbled, their only means of vision being headlights much reduced in power by the shields which provided only downward slanting slits of light. There was little chance of seeing pedestrians and even though there were much fewer cars on the streets then, particularly as petrol was rationed, the consequences were dire.

The authorities were not heedless of the situation. Kerbs were sometimes painted white, as were the lower parts of lamp posts. Drivers were compelled to have their bumpers and running boards painted white also. As a teenager living in Pellon, Joan Sutcliffe felt it wise to buy a 'glow worm' if she intended to go out after dark. This was a luminous badge which glowed in the dark once it had been held to the light to get it going. However it did not last too long, and the struggle between the pedestrian and the car remained an unequal one. Buses too could be a menace on the darkened streets, but travelling on one was at least safer than stumbling through the blackout on foot. Nevertheless it was a cheerless experience. Only a dim blue light issued from the heavily cowled bulbs inside, and the windows were painted dark blue, with sometimes a covering of anti-blast netting or glued on strips of paper. However it was better than nothing, and 'nothing' was what people locally got after 9 pm because of the bus curfew imposed by the Regional Transport Commissioner. This caused much ill feeling, leading to a protest petition in Halifax in January 1942 signed by 21,000 people. The authorities were not to be moved and it was not until June 1944 that the curfew was moved to 10 pm.

The most common experience of the blackout was that of getting totally lost in seemingly familiar surroundings, or of suffering some minor mishap. Vincent Holt was a schoolboy in Todmorden at this time and having visited the Hippodrome Cinema one night, he struggled through the blackout curtains of the exit door before, "striking out confidently for home." The next thing he knew he was waking up on the pavement, having walked straight into a lamp post.

Auxiliary Ambulance with regulation headlight blackout shields.
Courtesy of Calderdale MBC Libraries, Museums and Arts.

Vincent Holt….a painful collision in the blackout.

Harold Doyle and his wife also paid a visit to the cinema one evening, this time in Halifax town centre. The return home to Gibbet Street should have been straightforward, but it was not until they had reached King Cross that they realised how much the total blackness had disorientated them. Alice Beaumont was to recall the feeling of total helplessness as she groped her way home through the streets of Hebden Bridge one night. The absence of familiar landmarks meant that having reached her own street, she actually had to count off the doors in order to reach her own house.

Travel beyond Halifax and Calderdale during the blackout years was fraught with difficulties. In the first place the government was none too keen on what it regarded as frivolous journeys, preferring to preserve the railway system for the movement of service personnel and war freight. 'Is Your Journey Really Necessary?' was the question posed by posters displayed in bus and railway stations. If the 'you' in question decided that it was, the next problem was the destination. Buses only had numbers on the front, not place names.

Signposts disappeared from roads early in the war, not to reappear (in towns only) until October 1942. To further confuse German paratroopers, but also the British travelling public, town names were blacked out on shop signs; so, for example, the Huddersfield Co-operative Society simply became the anonymous 'Co-operative Society.'

Rail travel was an experience with a unique flavour. It could be regarded as an adventure or an ordeal, depending on whether one actually wanted to arrive at the right place at the right time. Alice Beaumont of Hebden Bridge found that trains were invariably packed with service personnel complete with packs, respirators and kit bags. Seats were at such a premium that during a long journey, the offer of a kit bag to sit on, or even the knees of a complete stranger, could not be dismissed lightly. A combination of black painted windows and missing station signs could turn the journey into a 'mystery tour,' so that alighting at the correct station depended on local knowledge or pure luck.

> *A train which passed through the Calder Valley one night must have provided its passengers with an extra 'frisson.' Drivers and firemen usually ensured that the engine cab had a covering which concealed the glow of the firebox, a precaution which had been neglected on this particular occasion. As a result, according to Harry Turner, who lived in a cottage next to Hebden Bridge railway station, the train was pursued by a Dornier bomber until it managed to find refuge in Summit Tunnel.*

Whatever the problems and difficulties caused by the blackout, the people of Halifax and Calderdale were soon left in no doubt that Air Raid Precaution Committees took their responsibilities seriously and that the regulations would be rigidly enforced. No matter how good their intentions, wardens became unpopular figures with their eternal cry of, "Put that light out," at least until the Hanson Lane bomb of November 1940 showed that there really was danger from above. The first local lighting prosecution came as early as September 12th 1939, when a trader on St. James' Road, Halifax, was fined £2. The court case suggests that he did not really take the new regulations seriously. In December 1939 came the first prosecution for careless use of a hand torch. During 1940 the number of blackout offences resulting in prosecutions escalated to a massive 1,700. At the heart of most of these cases lay carelessness, or momentary inattention, rather than a deliberate attempt to flout the law. Marjorie Brierley was an example of someone who had nobody at home to give her a reminder. Lodging in Gibbet Street, with her husband abroad in the Pioneer Corps, she simply forgot to turn off the light before opening the door, resulting in a fine.

Blackout awareness had to become a sixth sense, but it was also possible to develop a localised 'tunnel vision,' as exemplified by the old lady from the Midlands. At the height of the blackout, she went to the railway station to buy a ticket to go and see Blackpool Illuminations! One way or another the blackout had to be

endured until September 17th 1944, when it was replaced by the 'dim-out,' or 'half-lighting' as it was officially called. Householders could return to normal curtains and blinds, but direct lights outside still had to be avoided. The total ending of the blackout did not arrive until virtually the end of the European war – April 24th 1945.

This would have seemed a depressingly distant point in the future to those who endured the first blackout months and that first wartime winter of 1939-40. This was the phase known as the 'phoney war,' a time of seeming inactivity but also great uncertainty. Having attacked and overcome Poland, no one could be sure what Hitler would do next. All the same, the war itself must have seemed still a long way off as winter turned into spring in 1940. Suddenly, at the end of May, the war was on everyone's doorstep. Tom Lawlor, then a pupil at St. Mary's School, was not alone in witnessing a scene that was unforgettable among those who shared this memory – the sight of hundreds of tired, hungry and dirty soldiers being marched up Horton Street from

Halifax air raid wardens – tight on light.

Courtesy of Stephen Gee.

the railway station. The great evacuation from Dunkirk had just taken place and that ragged parade on the evening of May 31st 1940 was to be repeated constantly during the following weekend.

The events that triggered off the arrival of this tide of humanity at Halifax had begun with the dramatic ending of the 'phoney war' in Europe. In a series of lightning or 'blitzkrieg' attacks, Germany had quickly conquered Denmark and Norway in April 1940, before thrusting into France via Holland and Belgium on 10th May. On that very day, Neville Chamberlain had been forced into resignation and Winston Churchill became Prime Minister, promising nothing but, "blood, toil, tears and sweat." The 'bulldog' had been able to do nothing, however, to prevent German forces sweeping through France, although the 'miracle' of the Dunkirk evacuation had saved 338,226 British, French and Belgian troops, enabling them to fight another day. Among the gallant crews of the ships which went ceaselessly back and forth under heavy fire and aerial attack was Stoker Reginald Whiteley of Halifax, who received the Distinguished Service Medal for his exemplary conduct.

These, then, were the men that Tom Lawlor and many others saw marching up Horton Street – some of the remnants of a seemingly defeated army. They were, however, treated like heroes. A civic welcome awaited each newly arrived batch at Halifax station, and the crowds lining the streets were spontaneous and generous in their offerings of food, drink and cigarettes. The suddenness of the arrival of soldiers in large numbers, however, was difficult to cope with. Tom Lawlor saw the Moor at Halifax turned into a large open camp that weekend, with roped off sections for different units. Others were to be found on the square at Wellesley Park barracks. Crowds gathered at both spots, the adults to bring comforts, the kids to cadge strange looking French coins from the weary survivors.

The task of finding temporary billets for the Dunkirk evacuees until units could be reorganised was soon in full swing. Officers were generally found private billets whilst 'other ranks' were put up in mills and church buildings. Miall Street and Ellen Royd Mills, along with Brunswick Chapel, were used and the whole district threw its weight behind the effort. In Brighouse, for example, the Sugden

Dunkirk survivors in Halifax – the 'phoney war' was over.

Courtesy of Stephen Gee.

21

Memorial Hall, Bridge End, provided a reception centre, and after billets had been found it provided a social centre for soldiers. As with many other situations in the early stages of the war, dealing with this sudden military influx consisted of a mixture of precise organisation and random improvisation. Margaret Brennan, for example, helped out in a smooth operation whereby soldiers arrived at Woodside Baths, Boothtown, where they could bathe and receive clean clothing before being billeted around Range Bank.

A lady living on St Alban's Road, Halifax, saw the other side of the coin, whereby soldiers seemed to be wandering about seeking their own accommodation, with rank being no consideration. She returned from Heath School Sports Day to find two very dirty soldiers sitting on her doorstep pleading for 'digs,' as they had nowhere else to go. 'Taffy' and Stephen stayed for a fortnight and did not have too bad a time of it, even being taken to play a round or two at West End Golf Club. In return 'Taffy' left a grey blanket which had travelled through Belgium and France, but was now to serve the household for many years as an undercloth when ironing was done on the table.

No matter how brief the stay of the Dunkirk evacuees in the area, they themselves left the most vivid of impressions. Joan Sutcliffe, living at Albert Road in Pellon at the time, felt the tranquillity of a Saturday afternoon on the tennis courts charged with a sudden sense of urgency as the local vicar arrived and described the desperate plight of the soldiers now pouring into Halifax. Joan and her friends were given money to get bread and cakes from local shops to feed those who were arriving at St Hilda's Sunday School. Much of the food was given freely by the shopkeepers. This little cameo was more than just a fleeting and relatively trivial incident for two of the participants. It turned out that one of the tennis group ended up marrying one of the soldiers.

Meanwhile, down at Oak Terrace, off Hanson Lane, the residents were producing food and dragging out their tin baths for the soldiers who had just arrived at one of the Miall Street Mills. Mary Crossley, who as Mary Prout

had been on the Isle of Man at the beginning of the war and had hoped to be stranded there, was now reconciled to married life on Oak Terrace. She thought that the strangest sight of all was when one or two soldiers took off their helmets to reveal kittens brought all the way back from France. If that was heart-warming, then the condition of some of the soldiers showed what a harrowing ordeal Dunkirk really had been. Doreen Russell lived at Siddal at the time and virtually every house took in as many men as could be accommodated. As a 14 year old she was fascinated by 'Sandy,' who simply fell asleep instantly whenever he sat down. 'Sandy's' pal, 'Buster,' had managed to get a billet in Savile Park, but had arrived in Halifax with nothing but the clothes he stood up in, minus boots.

The Dunkirk experience seemed to have given a certain resilience to 'Buster,' billeted at Savile Park. When the air raid sirens went one night, and the lady of the house suggested that he should retreat from his bed to the cellar, 'Buster' (a good Yorkshire lad) replied, "Nay missus, wakken mi up when t'muck starts dropping."

And so the Dunkirk survivors came and went, and judging by the fact that the men of one large-scale billet gave a party for 300 children, they were grateful for the warmth of their reception in Halifax and Calderdale. In a way, so far as the war was concerned, the whole episode ended the 'age of innocence' for the locality. The war now seemed so much closer, had a harder edge to it. This new- found reality entered another dimension when the, "Wot no bombs?" phase ended. In late June 1940 a stick of eight bombs fell near the Gorple reservoirs. True they landed harmlessly on moorland, but it showed that the enemy was indeed up there. The all-conquering German armies also stood along the coastlines of France and the Low Countries poised for the next step, which would clearly be the invasion of Britain.

STEP FORWARD THE LDV

"You can always take one with you." Winston Churchill

Even before the fall of France in late May and early June 1940, the British were preparing to defend their homeland. The national mood was one of grim determination, a mood that was reflected in Churchill's, "We shall fight on the beaches" speech of June. As the German armies had poured through France in May, armed groups of civilians in the East and South-East of England had formed, and it was in response to pressure from below as much as to an initiative from above that brought a new home force into being. On the evening of May 14th 1940 the Secretary of State for War, Anthony Eden, made a broadcast in which he invited those thousands who had been asking what they could do, to join a new defence force which would be named the Local Defence Volunteers (LDV). The appeal was aimed at men between the ages of 17 and 65, and anyone interested was to register immediately at a local police station. That the appeal struck a popular chord is proved by the fact that within twenty-four hours 250,000 men had registered and police stations had been literally overrun. Within three days 800 men from Halifax and district had enrolled and other local police stations must have reflected the events at Todmorden where, on the evening of the broadcast, a bewildered police sergeant found his peace shattered by dozens of men clamouring to answer an appeal which he had not even heard. By the end of June 1940, the LDV nationally numbered 1,456,000 – a figure way above expectations.

At the outset the LDV had a very clear role. The invasion scare was compounded of two elements – a possible attack by German parachutists assisted by an internal 'Fifth Column' made up of spies and traitors. The LDV was created in order to combat both elements. The question was – how? The huge number of volunteers had caught the government 'on the hop.' The LDV lacked uniforms, weapons, a proper rank structure and

military discipline. What the LDV did have was boundless enthusiasm. Harry Leah of Todmorden was a 14 year old schoolboy in 1940, but his father immediately went to Manchester and purchased a .22 sporting rifle – all that was left at the gunsmith's shop. Not content with this, he bombarded the War Office with requests for a Lewis machine gun, which he intended to fix to his roof and shoot down enemy aircraft. Unsurprisingly, the War Office was deaf to his pleas.

Young Harry Leah, complete with .22 sporting rifle.

The only item of uniform at first available was a simple LDV armband. By the end of June khaki denim 'one size fits all' two piece overalls and service caps were arriving. There were no arms whatsoever. Large amounts of weapons had been abandoned on the beaches of Dunkirk, and the priority was to re-equip the regular army. Hence the LDV tended to do rifle drill with broom handles, and recruits armed themselves with knives, clubs, bags of pepper, cutlasses, shotguns and ancient weapons smuggled out of local museums. Not only this, the LDV consisted of those too young, old or unfit to be conscripted, and men from 'reserved occupations.' The emphasis was on older men, especially Great War veterans. Thus was born the image of 'Dad's Army' and tense though these days were, there were enough wits and wags about to find plenty of humour in the uniform, weaponry and elderly make-up of the early LDV – 'Long Dentured Veterans' as they were sometimes dubbed. Others saw this 'scratch' defence force as symbolic of a Britain that really was at the end of the road and interpreted LDV as 'Last Desperate Venture.'

The most acute problem was the lack of weapons. A few of the standard British army issue rifle, the .303 Lee Enfield, were available, and these were supplemented by hastily ordered arrivals from overseas. From Canada came 75,000 vintage World War One Ross rifles, and the USA dispatched a quantity of .300 Springfield and Remington rifles, about 100,000 in number, which had lain in thick yellow grease for twenty years. The government also requested that sporting rifles and shotguns should be handed in at police stations for LDV use, but by the end of June 1940, on average one rifle had to be shared by six men.

Nevertheless, low on weapons but high on enthusiasm, the LDV soon made its appearance in Halifax and Calderdale. On May 19th 1940, under the overall command of Colonel Raymond Shaw, the 21st and 22nd County Battalions of the LDV, attached to the Duke of Wellington's Regiment, came into being covering Ripponden, Todmorden, Hebden Bridge, Sowerby Bridge, Elland, Brighouse and Hipperholme. A special Railway Company of the LDV had responsibility for protecting the railway line from Elland to Hebden Bridge. A little later, two more West Riding battalions were raised, the 23rd and the 24th, to cover the old borough of Halifax, and again attached to the local Dukes.

The precise function of such battalions was laid down in a War Office pamphlet, which candidly admitted that the LDV had neither the training nor equipment to offer any meaningful resistance to highly trained German troops. Its role was to guard communication links, factories, reservoirs; in short, anything which might offer itself as a useful target to an invading force. However, observing and reporting, rather than fighting, were to be the key features of the LDV's duties. 'Look, Duck and Vanish,' perhaps the most dismissive and certainly the most famous of the nicknames attached to the LDV, in fact summed up precisely what was expected of the force in its early days.

And so they came forth, the youths and the veterans of Halifax and Calderdale and those who for any reason were unable to serve in the front line forces, ready and willing to do their duty. Young Vincent Holt's first sight of the LDV captured the mood of those early tense days of June 1940 – a lone figure with nothing more than an armband and a shotgun patrolling a reservoir at Blackstone Edge. Tension and suspicion were certainly in the air for Halifax man, Harold Akroyd, who was arrested by the police as he was mapping prominent landmarks on nearby Lindley Moor. It was useless to protest that he was doing this as a favour for the local commanding officer of the LDV, Colonel Raymond Shaw, and Harold was advised that he had better join the force if he wanted to avoid repeated arrests. Harold had an artistic and inventive streak which was to make him

H. AKROYD, SERGT. 'I' SECTION
HALIFAX SECTOR

Harold Akroyd's heraldry: the translation reads: "Perhaps one day it will be a pleasure to remember these events also."

The artistic Sergeant Harold Akroyd stands at far right.

useful to the force in unusual ways. One of his creations was a rifle range at Brookroyd Mills with moving targets – little figures which, appeared and disappeared at windows and street corners.

Lonely Bridestones Moor, high on the hills above Todmorden, was the scene of the first operational duty of the local LDV. On May 30th 1940, the Todmorden 'A' Company of the 21st Battalion performed a dusk to dawn watch, a duty that was repeated nightly until 'stand-down' in November 1944 at this bleak location commanding a view of the

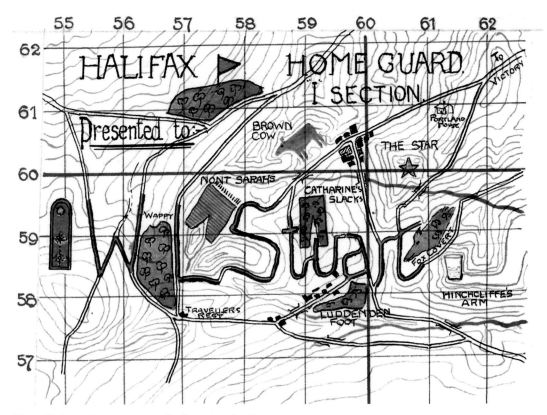

Akroyd's inventive map is worth close examination.

Long Causeway. Harry Leah joined 'A' Company, perhaps unofficially, as a schoolboy of 14. Even at that age he did his stint on night duty, and his father and others placed a wooden board showing the cardinal points of the compass on Bridestone Rocks. The timber has long since gone, but many years after the war, Harry himself was to chisel a simple inscription into Bridestone Rocks as a tribute to the nightly vigil of Todmorden 'A' Company.

Harry Leah's tribute to 'A' Company (Todmorden).

In keeping with the original aim of the LDV, reservoirs were focal points for the activities of the local volunteers. From Blackstone Edge and Widdop in the west, to Lands Reservoir (which disappeared at the building of the M62) at Rastrick in the east, these stretches of water were regarded as points where enemy invaders could get up to all sorts of mischief. Harold Doyle, who joined the LDV at the outset, found his night guard duties alternating between a local reservoir and Halifax railway station. He was rather bemused by the fact that his early training included the use of semaphore by flags – boy scout fashion. Raymond Dean, an apprentice boilermaker at Hartley's and Sugden of Gibbet Street, was often on LDV night duty at a reservoir at Pellon. He found himself slightly embarrassed at having to challenge people rolling home from the pub, and even more embarrassed at their unprintable responses.

Geoff Allinson was a resident of Pellon itself and an apprentice joiner at Johnny Blackburn's of Gerrard Street. He volunteered for the LDV as a 17 year old, joining 'B' Company of 23rd Battalion. Once a week his little party would meet at the New Inn, Mount Tabor, at 8 pm, imbibe a good deal of beer (if available) and then proceed to Fly Flatt Reservoir on the last bus. Here, Geoff's group would patrol the Withens Moor in pairs, armed at first only with sticks. When not on patrol they attempted to get some sleep in the tap room of the Withens Hotel, surrounded by stuffed birds, an experience almost as eerie as that of patrolling the bleak landscape outside.

Now picture another eerie scene. Young Ken Hirst is patrolling a dirt road between his command post at Horley Green Road, Claremount, and Stump Cross. He is an apprentice engineer and a proud member of the Home Guard (the new name suggested by Churchill in July 1940 to give a bit of 'zing' to the force) but it is dark and he is alone. Ken peers into the darkness and nervously clutches his rifle. The air raid siren has just gone and wisps of mist drift across the fields. Solitary trees easily transform themselves into ruthless German paratroopers. Ken walks forward a few steps and the crunch of his boots is echoed on the other side of the wall bordering the road. He stops; the other footsteps stop. He continues a few paces; the other steps continue. At last Ken decides that he must take action. He whirls around quickly towards the wall – "Halt, who goes there?" A loud neigh greets his challenge (or is it a laugh?) and at the same time the siren sounds the 'all clear!'

A smart looking Home Guard group at Hebden Bridge.

Courtesy of the Longstaff Collection

Stories such as this were multiplied a thousandfold across the length and breadth of Britain as the war progressed, bringing mirth in equal measure to both the tellers and the listeners. They evoked the 'Dad's Army' stereotype of the Home Guard, the one which predominates today. However, although the models for Mainwaring, Pike and Godfrey undoubtedly existed, it is a very skewed view. Hindsight offers us a simple interpretation. The German invasion never took place and the Home Guard scarcely fired a shot in anger. Who was to know this in 1940 after the way German troops had so easily overrun the Low Countries and France? There is plenty of evidence to show that the Home Guard took its duties very seriously in these early days. Not long after his encounter with the sociable horse, young Ken, on the same dark lane, had his bayonet no further than 25 cm from the throat of an approaching figure on a bicycle who seemed as if he was not going to stop at Ken's command. The figure turned out to be that of an air raid warden who complimented Ken on sticking to his duty.

It is unlikely too that those who did laugh at the Home Guard, did so openly. The consequences could be dire, especially if one decided to pose as a spy or 'Fifth Columnist.' Lewis Robertshaw, a youngster in Elland in 1940, soon learned of the fate of two prominent local councillors who had loudly and publicly proclaimed their disdainful opinions of "Saturday night soldiers." Having had rather too much to drink one night, they were challenged by two Home Guarders on duty at Elland gasworks. The flippant response from the boozy pair – "We are from Column Five. What are you going to do about it?" – did not go down well with two men who were voluntarily giving up a night's sleep every week. One of the councillors was dropped headfirst into a huge water butt, and having been rescued by his companion, the pair showed a little more humility as they quietly made their way home.

The self-esteem of the Home Guard was helped greatly as, from July 1940, proper equipment began to arrive in the shape of steel helmets, respirators, greatcoats, leather gaiters, boots, leather belts and haversacks. Weapons, however, remained a problem. The American and Canadian rifles were coming 'on stream,' but they were more than matched by the mushrooming numbers of volunteers. An issue of five rounds per man seems to have been standard for patrol or guard duties at first, although in the very early days it was not unknown for a patrol of eight to have five bullets between them. Nevertheless enthusiasm was not in short supply as the volunteers spent evenings and weekends getting to grip with foot and rifle drill, bayonet fighting, unarmed combat, map reading and lectures which included the vital skill of aircraft identification.

or ceiling as a novice felt the recoil of a rifle for the first time. Toothill Rifle Range served the Brighouse Home Guard and quarries all over Calderdale cracked to the sound of rifle fire. Hipperholme Home Guard, for example, used quarries beyond the Old Brodleians playing fields. At the other end of Calderdale, the Shepherd's Rest pub, on the edge of Langfield Moor, became a centre for the weekend activities of the Todmorden volunteers. A shooting butt was built across a narrow valley at which the local lads got plenty of practice. Interest was further maintained by the arranging of contests with neighbouring groups. Strangely, the Todmorden lads never seemed to lose and regular spectator, Vincent Holt, attributed this to the pub landlord plying the visitors with plenty of beer. "By the time they came to shoot they had difficulty getting down to the ground and even more difficulty getting up again."

Larger scale rifle ranges were to be found at Marsden, Huddersfield and at Oxenhope, which also had an extensive bombing range. The government was very keen on bombs and grenades for the Home Guard because, as opposed to rifles, they could be produced both quickly and cheaply. The first weapon universal to the force was the No. 76 Self-Igniting Phosphorous Grenade, otherwise known as the 'Molotov Cocktail.' Others to follow included the No. 73 'Woolworth' or 'Thermos Flask' Bomb, and the No. 74 'Sticky' Bomb. All these rather chillingly named grenades were supposed to be anti-tank weapons, but in truth they could all do as much damage to the thrower as to the target. The 'Sticky' Bomb, for

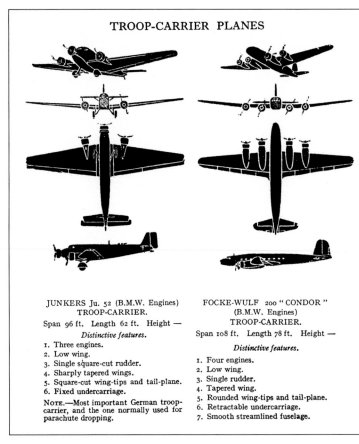

TROOP-CARRIER PLANES

JUNKERS Ju. 52 (B.M.W. Engines)
TROOP-CARRIER.

Span 96 ft. Length 62 ft. Height —

Distinctive features.
1. Three engines.
2. Low wing.
3. Single square-cut rudder.
4. Sharply tapered wings.
5. Square-cut wing-tips and tail-plane.
6. Fixed undercarriage.

NOTE.—Most important German troop-carrier, and the one normally used for parachute dropping.

FOCKE-WULF 200 "CONDOR"
(B.M.W. Engines)
TROOP-CARRIER.

Span 108 ft. Length 78 ft. Height —

Distinctive features.
1. Four engines.
2. Low wing.
3. Single rudder.
4. Tapered wing.
5. Rounded wing-tips and tail-plane.
6. Retractable undercarriage.
7. Smooth streamlined fuselage.

Silhouettes that all Home Guarders had to be familiar with.

Above all, rifle practice was the priority. The Drill Hall on Prescott Street had a miniature rifle range and many a bullet hit the upper wall example, had a nasty habit of sticking to anything but the tank!

The increase in weapons was accompanied by a change in thinking about the role of the Home Guard. To merely observe, report and guard was felt at a local level to be not enough, and it was pressure from below for a more aggressive role that persuaded the War Department to sanction more offensive action, such as the harrying of enemy tanks, from as early as July 1940. There was, however, deep unease in official circles by the autumn of that year that they might have created a 'Frankenstein's Monster.' The Home Guard lacked a proper command structure and military discipline. It also seemed answerable to no-one but itself. Internal stresses at a local level were produced when 'old sweats,' veterans of the Great War, seemed haphazardly at times to be placed under the control of the local headmaster or solicitor. Veterans were disinclined to obey orders they disagreed with and too much drill offended them. As one veteran from Todmorden said as, withdrawing from drill, he pulled a handful of medals from his pocket, including the DCM and the Croix de Guerre, "I didn't win these on a bloody parade ground."

Worse still, with the enemy parachutists and 'Fifth Column' scare virtually reaching hysteria point by the autumn of 1940, the Home Guard was setting up road blocks and conducting night patrols wherever it fancied. It recognised no uniform other than its own and, on the principle that spies might well be in uniform, identity cards were being demanded from even the police and the military. One army officer came to the grim conclusion that the first major battle on British soil would be fought between the Home Guard and the British Army! Matters came to a head when officious Home Guarders delayed a fire brigade on its way to the London 'blitz' at a roadblock. Added to this, Home Guarders were developing distinctly 'trigger happy' tendencies, culminating in the killing of an army officer and the slaughter of five civilians in a car. To ignore, or even simply to mis-hear Home Guard commands, now risked death.

Barum Top, Halifax, is the scene of this Home Guard parade.
Courtesy of Stephen Gee

These serious incidents took place well away from Halifax and shooting incidents diminished rapidly from November 1940 when, in response to the problem, the government placed the Home Guard under King's Regulations. This meant a proper rank structure, with military discipline. Nevertheless, the Home Guard remained determined to carry out what it saw as its duty, even if in a more controlled fashion. Ken Hirst, as a member of 'B' Company, 24th Battalion, saw hard evidence of this when on a joint exercise with the regular army. His section had set up a roadblock at Godley and had instructions to stop and search every vehicle. When an army jeep approached, and its driver seemed intent on driving through regardless, Ken's sergeant put a rifle butt through the windscreen. When the horrified Ken saw that the occupants had, "more gold shoulder braid than I had ever seen," he was expecting a 'rocket' for the sergeant. On the contrary, it was the driver who got the dressing down, whilst the sergeant was complimented on his action.

WE MUST NOT DROP OUR 'GUARD'

Exercises…and more exercises…

By the summer of 1941 the enthusiasm of the rank- and-file Home Guard was waning, along with its numbers. To many, the threat of a German invasion was well nigh over after Hitler had launched his armies against Russia in June. A trickle of new weapons was coming into play, such as American Browning automatic rifles and Thompson sub-machine guns, but the 'raison d'être' of the Home Guard no longer seemed to exist. The government was not so sure and Churchill in particular saw the continuance of the force as vital for maintaining morale and the martial spirit. As a result, the Home Guard was included in the National Service Act of February 1942 which affected all people between the ages of 18 and 60. Now men could be compelled to join the Home Guard where numbers were short, or not allowed to leave if already in. There was to be a maximum of 48 hours training per month and those failing to attend could be prosecuted.

So how to occupy a body of men, some of them now effectively conscripts, which no longer had a clear idea of its purpose? One solution was to simulate the real thing in the form of exercises, often in conjunction with regular soldiers. On Sunday afternoon, October 19th 1941, one of the earliest of these exercises

This German prisoner (alias Fred Jagger) seems not too unhappy to be in the hands of his plimsoll wearing guards.

took place. As part of a huge civil defence operation simulating 'blitz' followed by invasion, two Home Guard battalions defended Halifax from groups of saboteurs intent on destroying transport centres and electricity plants. Such mock battles could be conducted in deadly earnest and Ken Hirst took part in one during which a combatant with a broken leg was ignored so as not to give away the position. On the other hand they sometimes provided the opportunity for irresistible farce as the less enthusiastic were 'killed' all too easily (no doubt with the pub in mind) whilst the more eager miraculously 'rose from the dead' time and time again.

Uninvited elements could also complicate the situation, as in the 'Battle of Folly' during which 'German parachutists' advanced from Lumbutts, Todmorden, and attempted to drive down the valley to capture the main road at Castle Street, with another Home Guard group resisting them. The youths of the locality progressed from being mere spectators to becoming inextricably mixed up in the exercise, to the confusion of all. Some found themselves 'manning' (or 'boying') a machine gun at the Old Mill House, whilst others were taken prisoner. As an exercise, the result was inconclusive!

Mock battles could often intensify already existing local rivalries and as a result could become distinctly edgy. The 'Battle of Blackshaw Head,' during which the Hebden Bridge Company defended the village from assault by the Todmorden Company, was quite a venomous affair. Matters were not improved when the Hebden Bridge Home Guard was later detailed to capture the railway station at Cornholme. The Todmorden lads guarded the hillsides and awaited the advance. The Hebden Bridgers, however, chose the smart option and arrived by train, capturing the station "unopposed." Such was the ill-feeling engendered by this incident that a general brawl broke out and a minor stabbing led to the shedding of blood.

Members of 'B' Company, 24th Battalion, display an interesting array of weapons outside Shibden Hall

Interest in the Home Guard could also be helped along as the number and variety of weapons increased. Large quantities of sten guns replaced the Thompson sub-machine guns, and the nickname of the 'Woolworth Gun' speaks volumes about the sten gun's potential for cheap mass production. Vickers machine guns, although large and cumbersome veterans of World War One, provided opportunities for men to practise stripping and re-assembly. On the heavier side, the crude Northover Projector, little more than a tube on a tripod and manhandled by three men, could launch grenades. By 1941 this was already being replaced by the 'Blacker Bombard' or

Ready for action – the machine-gun section of Todmorden Home Guard.

Spigot Mortar, a fearsome anti-tank weapon weighing in at around 360 pounds and needing a five man crew. It had a reputation for unreliability, and at its first demonstration it apparently almost killed General de Gaulle. The Smith Gun was a later cheaper anti-tank weapon. By the end of 1942, then, although the Home Guard never counted itself as being fully equipped, it had come a long way from those early days of clubs and shotguns.

With the end of the mass bombing 'blitz' of Britain in 1941, the War Office transferred 50,000 army men from Anti-Aircraft Command to field forces. Here was a golden opportunity to demonstrate that the Home Guard did have a positive and useful role to play even though the initial invasion scare had passed, and by 1942 around 11,000 of the force were being trained as anti-aircraft gunners in Ack Ack Units. They were joined by members of the ATS (Auxiliary Territorial Service) and, sadly, this was no soft option. Local girl Nora Caveney from Walsden, aged 18, had left her job in a silk mill in Littleborough to volunteer for the ATS in December 1941. Operating a predictor at an anti-aircraft gunsite on the south coast, she was killed by a bomb splinter in April 1942.

Although odd anti-aircraft batteries were to be found dotted around Halifax and surrounding district, by far the biggest concentration of fire-power was to be found on the airy heights of Southowram. From 1941 a

'Z' Battery of 112 single ground to air rockets was set up at South Lane. By 1942 it had been moved to a second site because trials had revealed the possibility of aircraft flying below the battery. This second site was at Withinfields Camp, Law Lane, covering an area which is

---

"These 'Z' Batteries represented the cutting edge of anti-aircraft technology"

---

now occupied by the Fairfax housing estate. Here 64 double launchers packing a punch of 128 rockets in all, awaited the appearance of any German raiders. These 'Z' Batteries represented the cutting edge of anti-aircraft technology in 1942, further assisted by radar tracking. The radar site for locating the targets was situated at Spout House Lane, Hove Edge, opposite the Old Pond Inn. The present Warren Park and Bole Hill Park housing complex would have presented a very different picture in 1942 – simply a field covered by wire mesh on wooden frame supports. The control room was linked by telephone both to Southowram and a similar 'Z' Battery at Bradley Bar, Huddersfield.

Frank Roper joined the Brighouse Home Guard as a 16 year old in 1942, and was transferred to Southowram in 1944. Here he became part of 102nd Rocket Battery of the West Riding Home Guard, linked to the Duke of Wellington's Regiment. A battalion of Royal Artillery regular soldiers manned the site by day, and the Home Guard by night. Frank spent one night per week on duty, either on alert or asleep in a Nissen hut. Each launcher had a two-man crew, one of whom was directly linked by headphones to the control room at Hove Edge. Each rocket was about 4 feet 6 inches long, and weighed around 56 pounds. The Southowram 'Z' Battery personnel were able to spend at least one weekend on the East Coast of Yorkshire where they practised firing rockets over the sea.

In general, service in anti-aircraft units was not popular with members of the Home Guard,

Rockets were never fired 'in anger' at Southowram, but unfortunately one was launched by accident on one eventful night in 1944. Fuses were being tested on guide rails which normally held 'dead' practice rockets, but somehow a 'live' one had slipped on board. The rocket made a spectacular flight between two houses before embedding itself in a railway embankment in the vicinity of Cleckheaton or Thornhill, but it did not explode. The only casualty was the tester himself, who ended up in hospital with burns.

especially after conscription had been introduced. Nissen hut sleeping accommodation was very basic and absenteeism was high. Ken Hirst was not unhappy to be transferred to Southowram, but after some time he found tedium to be the main problem. He was grateful to be transferred yet again, this time to a Bofors Gun sited at Southowram to combat low flying aircraft. The idea that a 'Z' Battery was not a 'good deal' is borne out to some degree by the experiences of K.G. Sutcliffe. By his own admission, 'K.G.' was not cut out for the military life. In fact, as

---

"accused of threatening a major with a bayonet"

---

a young apprentice engineer engaged in war work in Halifax, he quickly gained a reputation as a firebrand by organising a two-day apprentices' strike on the question of 'status.' He saw it as no coincidence that shortly afterwards he received a writ ordering him to join the Home Guard. It wasn't too long before 'K.G.' was brought up on disciplinary charges, accused of threatening a major with a bayonet whilst on parade at People's Park. 'K.G.'s story of self-defence did not seem to 'wash' and as a punishment he was transferred to Ack Ack, or anti-aircraft duties at Southowram. In the event, 'K.G.' did not find life at Southowram too bad at all. At least some of his one night's duty per

Name .... *Hirst K. Y.*

Nat. Reg. No. .... *KENE 228/5*

NIGHT MANNING

You are detailed to No. ....*3*........ Relief, and your Duty Nights are shewn below. You will bring knife, fork, spoon, mug or cup, washing kit, and National Registration Card. You must always carry this Duty Card. If you lose it—ask for another.

Relief No.	MARCH	APRIL	MAY	JUNE	JULY	AUG.	SEPT.	OCT.	NOV.	DEC.
1	4 12 20 28	5 13 21 29	7 15 23 31	8 16 24	2 10 18 26	3 11 19 27	4 12 20 28	6 14 22 30	7 15 23 1	9 17 25
2	5 13 21 29	6 14 22 30	8 16 24	1 9 17 25	3 11 19 27	4 12 20 28	5 13 21 29	7 15 23 31	8 16 24	2 10 18 26
3	6 14 22 30	7 15 23	1 9 17 25	2 10 18 26	4 12 20 28	5 13 21 29	6 14 22 30	8 16 24	1 9 17 25	3 11 19 27
4	7 15 23 31	8 16 24	2 10 18 26	3 11 19 27	5 13 21 29	6 14 22 30	7 15 23	1 9 17 25	2 10 18 26	4 12 20 28
5	8 16 24	1 9 17 25	3 11 19 27	4 12 20 28	6 14 22 30	7 15 23 31	8 16 24	2 10 18 26	3 11 19 27	5 13 21 29
6	1 9 17 25	2 10 18 26	4 12 20 28	5 13 21 29	7 15 23 31	8 16 24	1 9 17 25	3 11 19 27	4 12 20 28	6 14 22 30
7	2 10 18 26	3 11 19 27	5 13 21 29	6 14 22 30	8 16 24	1 9 17 25	2 10 18 26	4 12 20 28	5 13 21 29	7 15 23 31
8	3 11 19 27	4 12 20 28	6 14 22 30	7 15 23	1 9 17 25	2 10 18 26	3 11 19 27	5 13 21 29	6 14 22 30	8 16 24

Intended absence (work reasons, or leaving district) must be notified in writing IN ADVANCE to your Relief Commander at address overleaf.

In the event of illness a doctor's certificate must be sent. Change of address of yourself or next-of-kin must be notified.

MAJOR A. LUMB, M.C., H.G., 102 W.R.C., A.A. Battery.

Ken Hirst's Night Duty Card for the 'Z' Battery at Southowram.

week was spent in the Packhorse and the commanding officer, Major Lumb, seems to have been a humane and tolerant man. According to 'K.G.,' Major Lumb had a large firebell installed at the Packhorse, and at the push of a button at his headquarters he could activate the bell and bring his men pouring out if an alert was called.

Raymond Dean's experiences were somewhat different in that he came across more of the military rigour that was associated with 'Z' Batteries. As a teenage apprentice, Raymond had been an early volunteer to the Home Guard, doing a regular night duty at a Pellon reservoir, but by the time he arrived at Southowram the first flush of enthusiasm had worn a little thin. His first encounter there with military discipline was not an encouraging one. Sergeant Ormerod, a regular who had been transferred from the military 'glasshouse' at Sowerby Bridge, was not impressed by the drilling skills of some of the Home Guard men on duty one night, including Raymond. Consequently they were marched back and forth along Law Lane until they got it right.

The sort of shine Sergeant Ormerod would have approved of.

Matters took a turn for the worse when the authorities tried to impose two nights' duty per week, one at the Hove Edge radar station and one at Southowram. Raymond did heavy manual work in a foundry by day and felt that one night was quite enough. He threw down a challenge by absenting himself from the second night and, although he was fined £2 10s, he felt that he had won a moral victory when the two nights per week scheme was dropped.

However, if this was a mere brush with authority, Raymond then proceeded to involve himself in a head-on collision with it. As fate would have it, a friend's birthday coincided with a Saturday night duty. After a heavy drinking session in the afternoon, Raymond

---

"late and drunk at Withinfields Camp"

---

arrived at the Packhorse in the early evening in such a drunken and dishevelled condition that one of the customers described him as looking, "Like a bloody German paratrooper who's been wandering about on the moors since 1940." After more beverage, Raymond arrived both late and drunk at Withinfields Camp. Major Lumb, appalled at the thought of a drunken soldier in charge of live rockets, promptly had Raymond put in the guardroom.

This was such an unusual event that nobody knew quite what to do with him and Raymond spent a bewildering night, being constantly re-awakened to be shuttled back and forth between the cell and the Nissen hut as different officers countermanded each other. As dawn broke, and a ferocious hangover set in, an ATS girl brought Raymond the last thing he wanted to see – a 'delicious' breakfast of liver and bacon. Still groggy, Raymond received a severe reprimand from a panel of three regular officers before being released to make the long and rueful walk back home from Southowram. The matter was not forgotten and Raymond never was to receive his service certificate.

An episode of this nature was rare, but one element of Raymond's escapade was forming a

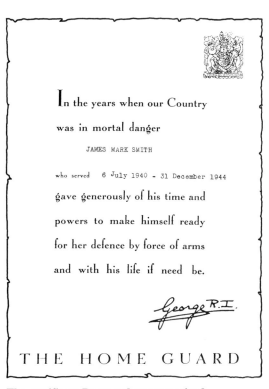

In the years when our Country was in mortal danger

JAMES MARK SMITH

who served 6 July 1940 - 31 December 1944

gave generously of his time and powers to make himself ready for her defence by force of arms and with his life if need be.

George R.I.

THE HOME GUARD

The certificate Raymond never received.

common thread through the Home Guard at large – a feeling of resentment at long working days accompanied by a seemingly purposeless night's duty once a week. By late 1943, with Italy out of the war and the Russians advancing from the East, the chances of a German invasion were regarded as virtually zero. Morale was dropping, especially among conscripts, and absenteeism was increasing. For men who had been in the Home Guard since 1940, night duty coupled with long working hours must have had a gradual wearing down effect, and it is worth noting just how long the wartime working week was. Ken Hirst, an apprentice engineer, stood at his machine from 8 am to 8 pm, Mondays to Fridays, and 8 am to 4 pm on Saturdays and occasional Sundays. Apprentices at his factory were not allowed to whistle or sing, and visits to the toilet were often 'spot checked' by the management. Ken did get some weekend time off for Home Guard duties, but his request to attend the weekend rocket-firing course on the

Yorkshire coast was firmly rejected by his management.

Employers, however, had their own point of view, and by 1943 they were becoming more vocal about the question of priorities. British industry was being asked to make an enormous effort to produce war materials. If there was no longer any real danger of invasion why, they asked, should the war effort be hampered by giving men time off for what now seemed to be purposeless activities? Why also should men have to arrive at work unduly tired once a week after a night duty that had become meaningless? In the face of all this, the War Office began to wind down Home Guard activities. All operational duties ceased from September 6th 1944 and the Home Guard was officially 'stood down' on November 14th 1944. It officially ceased to exist on December 31st 1944.

In London, on December 3rd 1944, King George VI, accompanied by the Queen and the two Princesses, took the salute at a grand 'stand down' parade as 7,000 members of the Home Guard marched past Hyde Park. Similar if smaller parades took place right across this locality. The Halifax parade concluded at Bull Green and in his speech to the 23rd Battalion, at the Regal Cinema, Colonel R.M. Shaw stressed the years of self-sacrifice, self-denial and self-discipline. The Home Guard was never

put to the test and it is difficult to assess how well it would have performed in the face of an invasion. The irony is that when the danger was at its height, the force was least well equipped to deal with it. As training and the supply of weapons improved, the danger receded. The 'Dad's Army' element was always there, but so too was a fierce determination not to knuckle under to oppression. In truth, however, its 'observing and reporting' function was probably more realistic than its eagerness to 'harry' the enemy.

Churchill was a constant supporter of the Home Guard as being good for morale and in his speeches he gave it as high a profile as he was able. He saw it as bolstering the mood of the nation and encouraging comradeship and loyalty within groups of men who might be called on to fight alongside each other. At a simple practical level, men who went on to be conscripted into the forces often found that the Home Guard had been a useful introduction into military training and the handling of weapons. Last, but not least, 1206 Home Guard personnel were killed on duty nation wide and 557 were seriously wounded. When it is considered that these casualties were sustained largely through accidents and not in combat with the enemy, it is clear that an element of danger did exist, and that it was not simply a matter of being "Saturday night soldiers."

NCO's of 'B' Company, 24th Battalion, ready to 'stand down' in 1944.

UNIFORMS – MANY VARIETIES

"Soldiers, soldiers everywhere…."

The Duke of Wellington's Regiment, now part of the Royal Armoured Corps, may have left Wellesley Barracks in August 1941, not fully to return until November 1946, but that did not mean the end of uniforms in Halifax and Calderdale. The Barracks itself became a training centre for the ATS (Auxiliary Territorial Service) and home to a detachment of Royal Engineers. The latter seemed to have used the local area as one huge training ground and dispersal centre, and they could be found from one end of Calderdale to the other. In Halifax itself they took over the Canal Dying building at Old Lane and the Alexandra Hall. Mills at Haley Hill were occupied by the Royal Electrical and Mechanical Engineers.

Range Bank Mills was a major centre for the Royal Engineers, and that they had come with the intention of staying some time was shown by the fact that the sergeants' mess was decorated in the regimental colours with painted cap badges on the walls. Mills, however, could be inhospitable places for housing large numbers of men, lacking in the sanitary and social facilities provided by permanent barracks. Many local people did what they could to compensate for this. These men were strangers, but part of a common cause and, after all, with many of their sons, husbands, fathers and brothers in similar circumstances elsewhere, the locals treated the newcomers as they hoped their own menfolk were being treated.

Margaret Brennan, for example, after her regular daily job at Paton and Baldwin's, woollen manufacturers, thought it no more than her duty to spend some evenings and Sundays as a volunteer in a canteen set up for soldiers from Range Bank Mills. Here they were provided with cheap buns, sandwiches, tea and a snooker table. A whist drive was enjoyed on Sundays.

The impact of the army was felt from one end of Calderdale to another. The mansion of

> *Joan Sutcliffe's family were regular attenders at St Hilda's Church, Gibraltar Road, and if anyone in uniform was in the congregation on a Sunday evening, Joan's mother would unfailingly offer an invitation to come home for supper. Perhaps this was in preparation for a trying day on Monday for, at least in the early years of the war, this was respirator practice day. All soldiers who went into Halifax had to wear their respirators, providing a rather eerie spectacle for the rest of the population.*

'Honest' John Fielden, nineteenth century cotton manufacturer and factory reformer, at Centre Vale, Todmorden, was occupied by the army, as was Openshaw's. In Hebden Bridge, soldiers were mainly housed in the empty Brown's Factory at the bottom of Moss Lane, although there were also detachments at Birchcliffe Sunday School and St Thomas' Roman Catholic Church Hall, Fairfield. Men in uniform hold an irresistible allure for children; strangers who have been to strange parts and sometimes speak in strange ways. So it was for John Tolley, a Hebden Bridge youngster who lived near Brown's Factory and found the Royal Engineers billeted there a source of constant fascination. They liberally distributed foreign coins to local children and even built a sledge for John when the snow came.

The fun really began when the soldiers departed from Brown's. The local kids, John included, found a way in and discovered case upon case of .303 rifle ammunition. Filling

> *"A fire was lit on spare ground and a handful of bullets was thrown in, to see what happened."*

their pockets, they took what they could away. With that cheerful disregard for danger which children often display, they prised the ends off bullets, poured out the powder and lit it. A disappointment – only a 'whoosh.' A fire was lit on spare ground and a handful of bullets was throw in, "to see what happened." Even by the standards of the most exacting child, the results were spectacular, with bullets flying in all directions. By a miracle no-one was killed, the only damage being to an office window in Mortimer's building yard. The boys that John ran around with were reckless, but not stupid, and they realised that they had better dispose of the evidence. Several cases of bullets ended up in the canal, and at least one took the long drop from Nutclough into the River Hebden. John later emigrated to Canada, but during one of his frequent visits home during the 1980s, the local press reported on mysterious finds of cases of bullets during the restoration of the Rochdale Canal. Feeling a trifle guilty, John decided to clear up the mystery at Hebden Bridge police station and escaped with a slight reprimand!

At the eastern end of Calderdale, the Royal Engineers moved into empty property in Hipperholme and Lightcliffe, including Crow Nest and Cliffe Hill Mansions. A Royal Army Ordnance Corps depot was set up at a former dye works at Birds Royd, Brighouse, comprising the factory itself and nine Nissen huts in the grounds. The officers' mess for the RAOC was at Toothill Hall, a private house off Huddersfield Road. The war also came to the Ryburn Valley in no uncertain terms, with literally thousands of troops based mainly at Kebroyd and Thorpe Mills, and Pancreol Works. Kebroyd provided a military training centre for the Royal Engineers. An assault course was created and the mill dam was utilised for the building of bailey and pontoon bridges.

The presence of both the Royal Engineers and the ATS at Kebroyd Mill and elsewhere in the Ryburn Valley, added an extra dimension to the social life of the area. Dances at Kebroyd, with music provided by an Engineers dance band, proved a great attraction to local girls. Once again, however, facilities were limited in some respects for the soldiers and the family of Dennis Greenwood provided a bath once a week for one soldier, then a bath for another

Church parades needed soldiers to look if they had stepped straight from Sam Stock's window.

soldier the following week. They were always the same two soldiers and Dennis' family got to know them very well. Many neighbours followed this practice, which helped to integrate the soldiers into the community. Dennis, a teenager at the time, pumped the organ at the local Thorpe Church, and on Sundays it was a very impressive sight to see an immaculately turned out body of men marching down on church parade from Kebroyd Barracks, led by the regimental band. It was a sign of those times too that the officers could carry out an inspection of maybe 500 men on the road outside Thorpe Church with little or no fear of holding up any traffic.

The billeting of soldiers in an area would have been viewed from a number of perspectives. Some would have seen them as a nuisance; some as an attraction; some as just one of those inevitabilities of war. However, the presence of soldiers in the Ryburn Valley must have brought comfort to all who saw more sinister indications that a war was on. At Cunning Corner a blockade against invading tanks was prepared, ready to be put in place speedily. The walls alongside the road were made higher and trenches were dug into the hillsides.

If the sight of soldiers became a familiar one in the locality, the war was still capable of springing a few surprises. The lead-up to 'D'-Day, on June 6th 1944, saw a gradual exodus of soldiers from Halifax and Calderdale as they

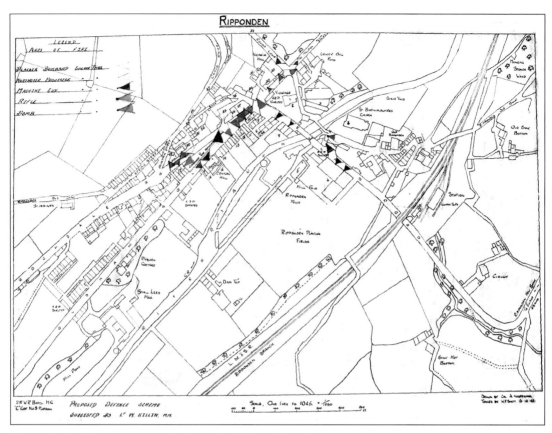

Ripponden's defences – as sketched by a local Home Guarder.

were called upon to join the big push. Quite suddenly, in late 1944, the eastern end of Calderdale seemed to be swarming with troops again. As Belgian towns and villages had been liberated, many young Belgians had volunteered to fight, and had been sent to Britain for training. It was part of this volunteer force which arrived in Hipperholme and Lightcliffe in late 1944, two companies attached to the Royal Army Service Corps – 1016 Company being Flemish speaking and 1018 Company French speaking. There was now plenty of property vacated by the Royal Engineers, including Cliffe Hill Mansion, Troutbeck House in Bramley Lane and the Manse of the Congregational Church.

Driving was one of the skills that the Belgians came across to acquire, and every night the village streets were packed with RASC lorries parked ready for driving practice the following day. Socially the Belgians were a

'hit' and the local girls flocked to the dances organised at the Conservative Club by a Mrs Longbottom and her daughter. Many friendships were formed this way, and also through the invitations to their homes generously offered by local families to the young Belgian soldiers. Here they enjoyed a little bit of the warmth of family life, along with whatever could be spared out of the families' meagre rations. Warmth was perhaps the key word, for 1944-5 was a harsh winter and the Belgians' billets in vacant property were, literally, freezing. In fact, 1016 Company virtually had to pull Cliffe Hill Mansion apart in order to procure enough firewood just to keep warm. Soon enough, however, the Belgians were able to join the final offensives into Germany, the only reminder of their presence being the word 'Belgique' carved into a tree along the drive leading to Cliffe Hill.

To all intents and purposes that should have

Norman and Joan Hopwood, third and sixth from the left, front row, enjoying the hospitality of Verbroedering, Lightcliffe in Belgium.

been that, but the young Belgians never forgot the hospitality they had enjoyed during that bitter winter of 1944-5 and there was a pleasant postscript. A small group of 1016 Company veterans, accompanied by their families, visited Lightcliffe in 1977. They had already formed an association called the Verbroedering Lightcliffe and they came again in 1978. In response, Norman and Joan Hopwood, Chairman and Secretary of the newly formed Lightcliffe Belgian Society, visited their counterparts the following year. This sparked off a series of alternating yearly visits between members of the two associations, which continued for around 10 years. The formal visits have now ceased, but friendships

and contacts are still maintained at a personal level.

To return to the wartime years, soldiers of a different type were to be found at Ovenden Camp, a convalescent and rehabilitation unit

Ovenden Camp convalescents at a party at Queensbury Cricket Pavilion

for injured or wounded soldiers. Their distinctive blue flannel jackets and trousers soon became a familiar sight around the place, with the Ivy House being their favourite 'local.' Their firing range, on the hillside at Bradshaw, ran from Oats Royd Farm to St John's Cross, and this 600 yards became a favourite spot for the local kids to trawl in search of live ammunition. There were about 1,000 men at Ovenden Camp, which covered the site of the existing recreation ground and whose road layout is still visible. The dances at the sergeants' mess figured prominently in the social lives of the local girls. As men approached recovery, the test as to whether they were fit to return to their units went, very loosely, as follows. The 'passing out' parade involved running from the camp to the top of Ringby Hill and back. Those who made it without passing out were considered fit to 'pass out!'

Servicemen of a different kind again were to be found at Sowerby Bridge – the 'bad boys.' When the siren went, the people of Sowerby Bridge realised that it was less likely to be signalling an air raid than to be warning of an escape from the military detention centre. The 'glasshouse' was situated in two empty mills on Walton Street, and the detainees paraded on an area that later became a cricket field. Habitual offenders were housed on the third floor to make escape attempts more difficult. The military staff in charge imposed a very harsh regime, the day beginning at 6.30 am with a physical training session on the parade ground. Everything inside – kit, equipment, walls and floors – had to be kept spotlessly clean. It was probably a welcome respite from the rigid discipline when the inmates came out to do snow shovelling in winter. Attempts to gain a more permanent freedom were not unusual, for these were men who were there for 'bucking the system.' The River Calder could be regarded as both an obstacle and an avenue to freedom. On one occasion an airman jumped in the river, only to become inextricably stuck in a mud bank. Another escapee, on a different occasion, managed to swim the river but was caught at the Friendly Pub.

> *The people of Sowerby Bridge regarded the 'glasshouse' inmates with a mixture of apprehension and curiosity as to why they were there. After 'D'-Day, in June 1944, there was a persistent story or rumour in the town that the detention centre was full of 'Red Beret' parachutists who had refused to jump.*

In the early years of the war, the uniforms that people most expected to see were those of an invading enemy. When at last a sight was caught of the enemy it was, unexpectedly, in the guise of prisoners-of-war. Jean Fields, a pupil at Holy Trinity School, Savile Park, saw prisoners working on nearby allotments, the large triangles on their prison dress indicating that they were 'safe' prisoners, allowed out to work. Jean's belief that they were Italians is partly borne out by a suggestion that it was Italian POW's who built Rye Lane in Halifax. John Tolley in Hebden Bridge regarded POW's working on the roads as a common sight, perhaps even more so just after the war. Many of them made clever wooden toys which they sold for a few pennies, and John himself had a wooden board with pecking hens for many years. It is more difficult to prove that there was a prisoner-of-war camp actually situated in the present area of Calderdale between 1939 and 1945, although suggestions have been made for Roils Head at Halifax and the grounds of Crow Nest Mansion, Lightcliffe. It is more than likely that the working parties came from camps outside the area.

There was, for example, a camp near Oldham and two escaped prisoners from there caused a minor stir in Ripponden in 1943. After the alert had gone out, an extensive search was carried out across rough countryside, but Lieutenant Wolfgang Kleibomer and Oberlieutenant Bernhard Scheers managed to snatch some sleep in a secluded field during the daylight hours. However, moving on under cover of darkness, they virtually walked into a roadside military guardroom and surrendered quietly when challenged.

GEARING UP FOR WAR

Essential Work Order 1941: engineering is classed as a 'defence industry.'

The enormous demands made in fighting the war, especially as it spread across the globe and brought in new enemies in the shape of Italy and Japan, meant that civilians had to become involved as well as the armed services. Total war meant that the industries of Halifax and district, in common with all the other towns and cities of Britain, had to make the war effort their priority. Working in war industries gave an individual the status of being in a 'reserved occupation' and hence safe from conscription into the armed forces. The most rational way to approach the massive war effort was to adapt the existing industries of an area to war production, and two of the major industries of this area lent themselves readily to adaptation – engineering and textiles.

The range of goods produced by a converted machine tool and engineering industry was truly remarkable. Churchill-Redman made searchlights. At Asquith's, another engineering household name, Harold Doyle made the metal parts for 'arresters' on aircraft carriers. His wife, Mary, worked a capstan lathe at Willis and Bates, Pellon, and helped to produce landing lights for airfields. That major name in carpets, John Crossley and Sons of Dean Clough, found their machinery turned to making webbing and bomb trolleys.

Halifax was considered to be a relatively safe area from the point of view of bombing and firms that had been bombed out elsewhere re-located in this area. Dean Clough housed Armstrong-Siddely from the Midlands which employed a local workforce to make sea and air torpedoes. Firth Brown from Sheffield also arrived at Dean Clough.

The story was much the same throughout Calderdale, with perhaps a wider variety of war work in progress. Helliwell's Patent Glaziers, at Birds Royd in Brighouse, belied the mundane innocence of its name by doing an astonishing variety of jobs, including straightening armour plate for tanks and making parts for bombs, landing craft and bailey bridges. A bombed out firm from London settled in Rastrick and its workers made wireless receivers for destroyers and parachutists. Meanwhile, at Sladdin's of Brighouse, aeroplane seats were made for the Royal Air Force. Brighouse in one respect was at the very 'cutting edge' of the munitions industry, for not only was Smith and Bulmer, at Bailiff Bridge, a Ministry of Defence explosives factory, but it is said that there was another one at Wakefield Road, near the present Armytage Industrial Estate. It was partly sunken underground between earth embankments, and the unfortunate workers there tended to gradually turn bright yellow from the handling of picric.

Business as usual at the Mackintosh factory.

At the other end of Calderdale came more examples of inventive adaptation. If the chicken firm of Thornbers, at Mytholmroyd, made arks for their poultry, then it was a small step to constructing Nissen huts. Again, the sectional buildings business of F.& H. Sutcliffe, Hebden Bridge, probably found it a straightforward task to make ammunition boxes. Not everyone had to adapt. Mackintosh's of Halifax carried on what it was good at – making sweets – but now mainly for the forces, to the tune of 10,000 tons in all. The confectionery element of the town's industrial make-up was augmented when the biscuit manufacturer, Meredith and Drew, moved to Halifax in 1940 as a result of the London 'blitz.'

No matter what the nature of one's work, this was a time for sealed lips. The fear of German spies and British 'Fifth Columnists' was so great, particularly in the early stages of the war, that it was felt by the government that even the smallest scrap of information might be valuable to the enemy. A comment about what one made at work might bring the bomber over or the

saboteurs in. A hint of where, say, a brother or boyfriend was stationed might lead to his death, and perhaps the same fate for others. 'Loose Lips Sink Ships' and 'Careless Talk Costs Lives;' these were the types of slogans with which the government hammered home the message on posters displayed prominently on the streets. Newspapers and cinemas were used to promote the same theme. Secrecy was all very well, but government propaganda gave no advice as to how certain people in Brighouse might try to explain away the fact that they had turned bright yellow!

Working days were long and hard. For those directly employed in defence industries, the working week was set at twelve hours per day, six days per week, with perhaps a little leeway on Saturdays for Home Guard duties. Striking was illegal. By the Essential Work Order of 1941, defence industries included engineering, aircraft production, shipbuilding, railways, mining and building. In these areas, workers could not leave their jobs without permission, a restriction that lasted until 1947, and the government had the right to direct 'essential' labour as it pleased. A worker could be fined for missing work without a doctor's note and, in extreme cases, could be jailed for persistent lateness.

The government meant business, and in August 1942 a Halifax man was sent to prison for this latter offence. In June 1943 a dairy hand at Halifax Dairies, Queens Road, was given a

---

"a month in prison for absenteeism "

---

month in prison for absenteeism. The long working day was fairly relentless, for as Harold Doyle, working at Asquith's found, the canteen carts came round once in the morning and once in the afternoon, but he had to snatch his 'cuppa' whilst still working his machine. There were of course, one or two 'silver linings.' Unemployment disappeared virtually overnight, and as Geoff Whiteley found out whilst working as an apprentice at Whitley's

You never know who's listening!

A message which needed to be heeded.

Textiles of Hanson Lane, although he couldn't leave his job, he couldn't be sacked either. For being 'cheeky,' he was merely sent home for three days – no doubt without pay.

The government was keen to show that although peacetime luxuries were disappearing in order for the country to gear up for war, the sacrifices really were worthwhile. Hence, in a Board of Trade poster it gave examples of unlikely conversions. Corsets were becoming parachutes and chinstraps; lace curtains reappeared as sand-fly netting; toilet preparations were transformed into anti-gas ointments. It was a simpler matter for one of the staples of local manufacturing. Textiles for civilian clothing switched readily to making uniforms, a process that in any case was not new to the district. Over two million uniforms were made locally in the course of the war. Harella made RAF uniforms. Victoria Mill, in the Ryburn Valley, provided yarn for RAF shirts and was so busy that the delivery date was eighteen months and order books had to be closed from time to time. Anyone working on such government contracts was in a 'reserved occupation,' with all the benefits and restrictions that this implied.

Above all, the Admiralty seemed to have a special link with Halifax and Calderdale. Away at Walsden, Harvey's were making 'navy blues.' At both Mytholmroyd and Hebden Bridge duffel coats for the navy were being produced at Redman's. Colin Wakefield's father worked for Priestley Bros. at Friendly, Ovenden, a firm that busied itself manufacturing blankets for the forces and duffel cloth for the navy. Royal Navy supply and storage depots were dotted around the area.

One person who saw the workings of the Admiralty at first hand was Kathleen Heys. She left Holywell Green School at the age of 14 and, unable to take up a secondary school scholarship, worked for a short time in a mill before becoming an office junior in 1943 at the head offices of the Naval Victualling Department in Halifax. The Admiralty had moved this department from Plymouth, partly to escape the heavy bombing there, but also to be close to the textiles industry which was producing so much of the navy's war needs. The offices where Kathleen had to solemnly sign the Official Secrets Act took up the entire floor above the well-known sports shop of Nicholl, Brown and Coyle. From these headquarters, the Naval Victualling Department administered the Yorkshire depots where stocks of food, clothing, and other equipment (other than weapons) were kept. Locally, radio equipment was stored at one of the Ryburn Valley mills. The main depot was to be found at Stainland, with yet another depot at Shaw's Mill, Holywell Green.

Kathleen was in the Issue Branch at head office, and one of her jobs was to deal with the post which accompanied the clews (or balls of yarn) and lanyards which were dispatched to HM Prisons to be made into hammocks – an interesting variation on the mailbags theme. Another of Kathleen's tasks illustrates how this war, in spite of all the strictures about secrecy and security, was sometimes pursued with an odd casualness. She was frequently sent down to the Rail Transport Officer at Halifax station, totally unescorted, to deliver bills of lading and documentation for supplies sent out from the Yorkshire depots to ships at home and abroad. This would have been dangerous information had it fallen into the wrong hands, but perhaps Kathleen offered the best security of all. Who would have suspected a young teenager

When one of Colin Wakefield's uncles, a sailor, arrived at the family home in Halifax, he was clad only in vest and trousers, with a blanket around his shoulders. His ship had been lost in the North Sea, and having been landed at Newcastle as a survivor, he had been given a travel warrant and sent on, as he stood, to his nearest relatives, the Wakefield family. He was able to get himself re-equipped locally through a Royal Navy storage depot before moving on to his own home in Birmingham for two weeks survivor's leave.

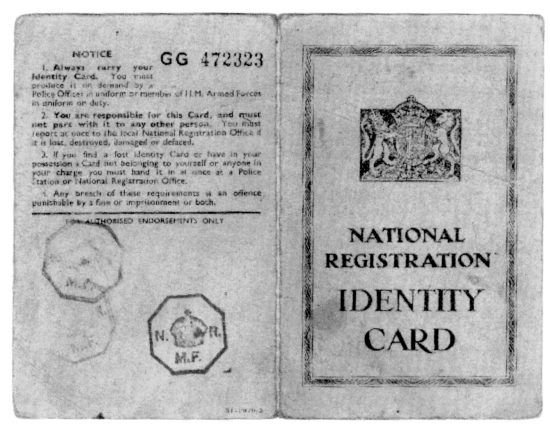

Wartime ID – had to be carried at all times.

wandering down Horton Street of carrying such crucial information?

In the three years that Kathleen Heys worked for the Admiralty at Halifax, before the offices were closed down and the Naval Victualling Department returned to Plymouth in 1946, she encountered a rich array of characters. Her immediate boss, Miss Booth, tended to defy convention by wearing rather racy coloured stockings. Mr Pengally, with the wonderfully West Country sounding name, delighted all with his green plus fours and purple socks when he breezed in from Plymouth. The three office juniors were totally taken in by the lurid story that Mr Martin, recently arrived back in England from the Gold Coast, was afflicted by an insect that had burrowed into his skin there. It ceaselessly journeyed about his body, and the only chance he had of removing it was when it passed across one of his eyeballs! Professor Wagg was the epitome of the English eccentric. A brilliant man, in charge of the six inspectors who looked after quality control at the local depots, he was one of the few people to have mastered the art of riding a bicycle in the rain whilst holding an umbrella over his head.

STEP FORWARD THE WOMEN

By 1943, 90% of women were doing work of 'national importance.'

Just as a generation earlier, during World War One, women had stepped out of the kitchen and into the workshop, their successors followed them, but with a difference. December 1941 saw the first ever female conscription in Britain, a sober indication of what 'total war' really meant in terms of civilian involvement. Whether enforced or not, whether enjoyed or not, women's contribution to the war effort was massive, encompassing the forces, war work, the voluntary services and the less than glamorous role of struggling to bring up children under a regime of strict rationing, with their menfolk absent. There is no doubt, however that in the eyes of the government the most urgent role for women was that of taking over the jobs that men were vacating through conscription.

By the autumn of 1941, the upper age limit for male conscription had been raised to 51 years. In December 1941, unmarried women and childless widows aged between 19 and 30 became liable to the call-up. In July 1943 the so-called 'grannies call-up' was imposed, by which women up to the age of 50 had to register for war work, although it was promised that no woman would be forced to neglect her family. By 1943 the astonishing figures of 90% of single women and 80% of married women were in some kind of work of 'national importance.' A woman could choose between three options – the forces, the Land Army or industry. A female householder could make herself ineligible for conscription by taking in an evacuee or a billeted soldier. It is true to say, of course, that women were voluntarily moving in to fill the gaps left by departing men, or to take advantage of new opportunities, before conscription was introduced. The female branches of the armed services, for example, were filled by volunteers. However, voluntary or otherwise, women soon found themselves doing a range of jobs that would normally

have been regarded as 'men's work' – driving mobile cranes, operating steam hammers, blacksmithing, chimney sweeping and acting as electricians, plumbers' mates, postwomen, 'clippies,' railway workers, motor-cycle messengers etc. Men's work – yes; alas, not men's pay.

WOMEN OF BRITAIN
COME INTO
THE FACTORIES
ASK AT ANY EMPLOYMENT EXCHANGE FOR ADVICE AND FULL DETAILS

This graphic invitation inspired a tremendous response.

As for Halifax and Calderdale, women were well represented in textiles before the war, but now they were able to play their part in an engineering industry put on a war footing. Marjorie Talbot and Vera Blenkinsop, for example, both found themselves making parts for air and sea torpedoes for Armstrong-Siddely, which had moved to Dean Clough from Birmingham. Movement was not all one

Cheerful war workers at Ormerod's, Hebden Bridge.
Courtesy of the Longstaff Collection

way. On December 15th 1941, the Mayor of Halifax, Alderman Percival Whitley, gave a civic send-off to 104 women from Halifax, Brighouse and Huddersfield as they departed in a convoy of special buses from Bull Green to work in a Royal Army Ordnance Factory in Staffordshire. Munitions work was now devouring both manpower and womanpower. An industry which had employed around 1.25 million people in 1939, it peaked in 1943 at around 8.5 million. So urgent was the call from Ernest Bevin, the Minister of Labour, that these women agreed to go before Christmas, having originally intended to spend the festive season at home. One woman, leaving her husband behind, had worked for 17 years in a cotton mill, but now clearly felt that her duty lay elsewhere. Mobility was one of the key elements of the social upheaval of the war years and, incredibly, there were over 60 million civilian changes of address.

Another former cotton mill worker, this time a machinist from Todmorden, found herself as one of the 100,000 or so women employed on the railways. Approaching this change with some apprehension, she soon got into the swing of things, literally, as she loaded and unloaded railway wagons for five years from 1941. Cotton, tea and cocoa seemed to constitute the

bulk of her work and, although it was hard labour, she never contracted a cold even though she had to work out in all weathers.

One Halifax woman thoroughly enjoyed her work as a bus conductress or 'clippie.' She must have brought out the best in her passengers, for she often got gifts from them, or even goods in part payment for fares. One of her regulars became quite concerned when, not displaying her usual cheerful disposition, she collected her fares with tears rolling down her cheeks. The mystery was solved when she pulled two onions out from her top pockets, a gift from a previous passenger – and in these days of absolute scarcity, this was a rare gift indeed. The appearance of women in an unfamiliar role was not welcome to all. Vincent Holt witnessed a very tense argument at a Todmorden bus stop between a loud, elderly man and a female bus driver. He refused to board the bus, claiming that, "This bloody strippet'll kill us afore Hitler does." She responded with plenty of spirit, and left him standing at the bus stop as she drove off to the cheers of the bystanders.

Women stepped into 'men's shoes' in all sorts of ways, sometimes with a good deal of reluctance. Phyllis Stead had only married her husband, Ronald, in 1940, and then he was called up later the same year. This left her to run their butcher's shop at Pye Nest on her own. She spent the next five years cutting and carving, lifting and carrying, rationing and regulating. She was mightily relieved when her husband returned so that the 'one woman show' could become a true family business again. On the other hand, Daisy Uttley quite enjoyed the war work that she did at Hartley's sewing shop, in Hebden Bridge. With a young daughter at home, Daisy was quite entitled to regard her workshops, the girls at Hartley's used the noticeboard to display letters from servicemen who had been former workers there, and proudly put up a large map on which to trace the progress of "our boys."

Something else that was a common theme of the time was the fact that Daisy put her young daughter, Kathleen, in the care of an aunt whilst she herself was at work. Day nurseries were not plentiful, and creches at factories even rarer. Most women with young children who went out to work relied heavily upon relatives and neighbours for childcare. The Mayor of Halifax, Alderman Percival Whitley, alluded to this in December 1941, at the departure of local

The last bus

The Conductress is responsible for the amount of passengers carried and that limited number must not be exceeded only under severe penalty. Be well-advised and return by an early bus. It is better for all.

Head Office: WALNUT STREET, HALIFAX

HEBBLE

BRITISH BUSES

Trouble on t'buses.

The Mayor of Halifax in December 1941, Alderman Percival Whitley.

upbringing as the priority, but when the works manager asked her to step in to relieve a shortage of manpower, she felt that she ought to "do her bit." The work was quite heavy, and it included putting out piles of cloth for machinists, but she enjoyed the companionship. In a scenario that must have been repeated in many factories and

women to work at the Royal Army Ordnance Factory in Staffordshire. Whilst congratulating them on their patriotism, he was not slow to point out that their leaving created problems for hard pressed local factories in meeting their labour needs. It was in this context that he announced the opening of Craigie Lee, Halifax's first day nursery and expressed his hope that this would encourage married women with children to fill the gaps.

The take-up of nursery places at Craigie Lee - accommodation for 45 five year olds and under – was, in fact, disappointing. There were complaints throughout the war of low take-up of places at other day nurseries too. At first sight this seems strange, for the fees – usually one shilling (5p) per day – appear to have been modest. To put this in perspective, however, when Marjorie Brierley's husband was called-up into the Pioneer Corps in 1941, her service allowance was seventeen shillings and sixpence (87.5p) per week and seven shillings and sixpence (37.5p) for her baby. Alice Beaumont, living in Hebden Bridge, got roughly the same allowance from the RAF. The normal working week was six days, and so six shillings for day nursery fees was a not inconsiderable amount, especially in view of the fact that Marjorie Brierley paid six shillings rent per week for a house on Gibbet Street. Mothers taking up the challenge of going out to work may have got a better deal financially out of relatives or neighbours, or they may simply have preferred leaving their little ones with people they knew and trusted.

Wives of the lowest ranking servicemen, with small children and no income other than the service allowance, were often in desperate straits. The rising tide of public resentment about this took some time to seep into official circles, but by 1944 the allowance for a mother at home with her serviceman husband away

"often in desperate straits"

was raised to the reasonable amount of £3 per week. By this time, too, the ordinary soldier was receiving three shillings per day, an increase of a shilling.

For some women, mainly young and unmarried, when the call came to do something outside the home for the war effort, or when conscription enforced a choice, they saw it as an opportunity to do something totally radical and different. They opted for the Women's Land Army.

Lady Bingley addressing Land Girls in stylish mode.

Courtesy of Stephen Gee

'Back to the Land, we must all lend a hand,
To the farms and the fields we must go,
There's a job to be done,
Though we can't fire a gun,
We can still do our bit with the hoe.'

Was it really a deep-seated urge to return to one's roots; the catchiness of the official Land Army song; or a recognition of the urgent need to raise food production as German 'U'- boats wreaked havoc on Britain's food imports? For whatever reason, the call to join the Land Army was a great success and by 1943, the peak year, about 80,000 young women had donned the rather stylish 'dress' uniform of a green jersey, corduroy breeches and a brown felt slouch hat. The Women's Land Army spread across Britain and engaged itself with anything to do with farming – ploughing, threshing, milking, thatching, poultry-keeping, shepherdessing and even rat-catching. The Timber Corps absorbed 6,000 of the volunteers.

If it was a change of scenery that the girls wanted, they certainly got it, for they were usually stationed away from home. Land Girls worked in Calderdale, for Lewis Robertshaw's mother kept a boarding house at Elland in which two Land Girls stayed. They worked at Morton's Farm at Elland Bridge. Local volunteers, however, tended to find themselves in what would then have been regarded as far-flung places, having their first taste of heavy outdoor work and living away from home. One volunteer from Todmorden found herself engaged in the back-breaking task of potato-picking at Spalding, Lincolnshire, in a field so long that she could not see the end of it. The 'friendly farmer,' following on in his tractor, threw baskets at the girls if he deemed that they were slacking.

A Queensbury girl had a similar experience, except that she started her potato picking, near Ripon, on such a cold October day that it was snowing. The girls plodded on, too stubborn to admit defeat. Undoubtedly it was heavy and hard work, but it was an adventure too, and for most of the girls, it provided an exhilarating feeling of independence. They often lived in hostels, and through living and working together, lifetime friendships were sometimes forged. The Todmorden volunteer was

Land Girls toiling in the fields near Hebden Bridge.

Courtesy of Stephen Gee

homesick at first, but soon found that the healthy open-air life suited her, as did the weekend dances at US air force bases, so much so that she began to stay at Spalding even during the holidays, feeling now that Todmorden was just too quiet.

Another of the Halifax volunteers never had any doubts from the start, having been put on a farm at Birdforth, near Thirsk. She was only 17 and rejoiced in the fact that she was allowed to drive a tractor and learned how to plough with a pair of horses. The stylish Land Army uniform was not always the most practical mode of dress for this type of work and more

the ponycart to Thirsk market on a summer's day, to sell butter, eggs and poultry?

Not all Land Army work was as orthodox as this. One local girl ended up as a rat-catcher in Cornwall, using gin traps and poison, a task she seemed to have enjoyed. More surprisingly, another found herself in North Wales supervising a group of female inmates from a nearby mental health institution who came daily to work on the land. They cleared thistles and stones, but were in the habit of wandering off to look for cigarette ends when they felt so inclined. So variety could be the spice of life for a Land Army girl. This fine army of 80,000

A happy Land Army wave – but strictly working dress.

Courtesy of Stephen Gee

often than not a pair of wellingtons, 'bib and brace' overalls, a heavy waterproof coat and a headscarf or turban was the order of the day in winter. However, to compensate for this, what could have been nicer than the weekly trip in

or so young females helped to push up the output of British agriculture by 70% between 1939 and 1943, as the acreage under plough was increased from around 13 million to roughly 19 million during these years.

WELCOMING STRANGERS

August 1st 1939 - proposed evacuee numbers for the Upper Calder Valley and Ryburn Valley 'reception area' – 5,750.

On Friday, September 1st 1939, two days before the official announcement of war, a train pulled into Hebden Bridge station containing 241 children aged between 5 and 14 years and a handful of teachers and mothers. Another batch arrived the following day, making a total for the two days of 353 unaccompanied children plus 100 pre-school children, parents, teachers and helpers. All these were billeted in private homes in Hebden Bridge, Mytholmroyd, and Cragg Vale. Trains stopping at Sowerby Bridge and Todmorden that weekend discharged similar groups. These simple local passenger movements, mirrored right across the country, symbolised a profound change in social policy. For the first time in history, a British government was organising the mass evacuation of children from urban areas to protect them from enemy bombing.

The image of groups of children on railway platforms tagged with labels, carrying scraps of luggage and their favourite toys, is one of the most enduring of the war. It is often made all the more poignant by the juxtaposition of the distressed faces of mothers with the smiling faces of the younger ones, believing it all to be one great adventure.

Plans had been laid down a year earlier, after the 1938 Munich Crisis. The country had been divided into three zones – 'evacuation,' 'neutral' and 'reception.' In the event of war, all schoolchildren and mothers with children less than 5 years of age, were to be moved from the evacuation to the reception areas. The plans were thorough; the registration of those eligible less so. It was soon known that the Upper Calder and Ryburn Valleys had been designated as a reception area.

One can imagine the thoughtful silence which fell on the various local council meetings when, on August 1st 1939, the numbers of evacuees the government proposed to send to their areas were announced – Todmorden 2,000, Hebden Royd 1,750, Sowerby Bridge, 1,100 and Ripponden 900. Evacuation Committees had already been formed and billeting officers appointed. The chairman of the Hebden Royd Evacuation Committee was Councillor E.B. Gibson, and as early as May 1939 his Chief Billeting Officer, Mr A. Spencer, had reported that 982 local households had volunteered to take evacuees. With the appointment of Mr E. Rushworth, the

"each child was given a bag containing 24-hour emergency rations"

headmaster of Central Street School, Hebden Bridge, as the De-Training and Transport Officer, all was in place as that train rolled into Hebden Bridge on the first Friday in September.

A well-rehearsed operation swung into action. Out of the 241 children from St Patrick's Elementary School, Bradford, 88 were swiftly transported to Mytholmroyd in four double-decker buses. The rest proceeded to the Co-operative Hall, in Hebden Bridge, where a meal was provided. Numerous volunteers helped with the communal feeding, and each child was given a bag containing 24-hour emergency rations – biscuits, corned beef and tinned milk. Billets in private houses had been allocated to the evacuees and there were no reported accommodation problems.

The first wave of evacuees across the country was not exactly a tidal one. Registration of mothers and children was inadequately done and there was no compulsion on those registered to actually go. Of the four million planned for September 1939, only about one and a half million

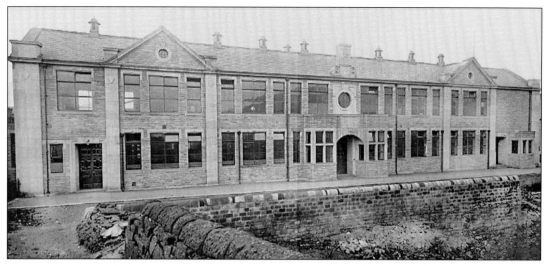

Hebden Bridge Grammar School – its numbers swollen by Bradford evacuees in 1939.

Courtesy of the Longstaff Collection

evacuees left the urban areas. This was reflected locally, and out of the many hundreds expected at Hebden Royd and Sowerby Bridge stations, slightly less than 600 actually arrived at the beginning of September. Nor had they come very far – only from Bradford – and the total by the end of the month for the entire local reception area was only 1,666.

This was no bad thing for local organisers, for it allowed them to have a trial run with modest numbers. A smooth integration into local schools was regarded as essential. In the case of Hebden Royd, the largest groups of children had come from St Patrick's Catholic Elementary School and Belle Vue Girls' High School. Whereas younger children were absorbed quite easily into a number of local elementary schools, all the Belle Vue pupils had to enter into the only secondary school in the area – Hebden Bridge Grammar School. Luckily, the pupils of Belle Vue Boys' High School had 'de-trained' at Sowerby Bridge, whilst 94 from All Saints School, Bradford, had gone to Ripponden. Even so, by the middle of September 1939, the Headmaster of Hebden Bridge Grammar School, Mr Herbert Howarth, was reporting almost in desperation to the local council. The influx of 98 girls from Belle Vue, plus 28 from other schools, had coincided with the largest number of local pupils ever enrolled – 204. The evacuee pupils had teachers with them, but space was so short that Mr Howarth could only contemplate a two-shift system or a take-over bid for either the Little Theatre or the Trades Club, just opposite the school on Holme Street. The first local evacuation crisis had arisen!

It was not to last. As the first weeks of war passed, and the bombs did not fall on Bradford, evacuees began to trickle back home. Bradford was too near for many parents to resist the temptation to come and collect their children. One or two of the latter even set off to walk home themselves. The 'phoney war' made some people wonder what all the fuss had been about and of the 1,666 local evacuees, only 286 remained by Christmas 1939. Hebden Bridge's initial figure of 453 was down to a mere 20 by May 1940. Perhaps there were many sighs of relief from Evacuation Committees across the land, for the trend to return home had been a national one. However, some suspected that all this had merely been a practice run, and that worse was to follow, much worse. The following years were to prove their suspicions well founded, but what no-one could predict was the degree to which the evacuee experience was to prove such a life-changing event for so many people, not necessarily for the worse.

A few years ago in Brisbane, Australia, Stan Pierce was leafing through a Yorkshire magazine which his brother had sent from England. A certain photograph suddenly transfixed him– a picture of stepping-stones across a stream running through woodland – and he was overwhelmed by emotion. Stan was immediately transported to 1940 and a succession of images – his home in Jersey Road, London reduced to a pile of rubble, with his red pedal car lodged somewhere near the top; a long journey north by rail and a 'sing-song' in the waiting room at Crewe; finally, an arrival at a row of cottages near a stream running through woodland, with stepping stones across.

Stan had arrived with his mother in Hardcastle Crags, near Hebden Bridge. Aged five, he spent only a year there before they returned to London, but even so he never forgot his "heaven on earth." Stan's Arcadia included sledging in the winter, gathering masses of wild primroses in spring and picking bilberries in summer. In lyrical terms he later described the walk to the little school he attended, through fields whose flowers provided an "artist's

palette" of colours. The power of these memories was such that they were to provide Stan with a refuge in the mind whenever he encountered later disappointments. Little wonder then that, almost 60 years on, a photograph in a magazine should have sent Stan into such a tumult of emotions.

Stan was part of that voluntary and largely unplanned migration from London which was triggered by the onset of the 'blitz' in September 1940. If the 1939 wave had been a 'phoney evacuation,' then this second wave, gathering pace as the 'blitz' was extended to other cities, was for real. Evacuees came from much further afield than Bradford, and there were no easy routes back home. The distinction between 'reception' and 'neutral' area now began to blur, a process which had already happened in Halifax and Brighouse even before the 'blitz.' At 5 am on June 24th 1940, 400 tired and bewildered Channel Islanders arrived at Halifax station, and a further 151 at Brighouse. They had been travelling for two days and nights, leaving so hurriedly to escape the Nazi occupation that they carried few possessions with them. Amongst them were Tommy and Nora Edwards with their children, Jeane and

Hardcastle Crags – forever in Stan Pierce's memory.

Courtesy of the Longstaff Collection

Stan Pierce and family in his "heaven on earth."

Peter. They had caught the last boat to leave Guernsey, the 'Hantonia,' and Tommy had simply abandoned his Austin 7 on the quayside. Councillor W. Lees, and a hastily mustered band of volunteers, met the refugees at Halifax station, and he described them as presenting, "a pathetic picture."

This was now the 'crunch.' No carefully laid out plans or registrations here, simply a group of 551 men, women and children who had descended on the district at very short notice.

Guernsey evacuees Tommy and Nora Edwards in 1941, with children Jeane and Peter.

They needed accommodation urgently, a problem compounded by the fact that they were families rather than simply children. However, the recent influx of soldiers evacuated from Dunkirk had given some invaluable experience in such matters. The Halifax group was transported by a fleet of buses to the Gibbet Street Institution, where hot meals and temporary accommodation were provided. The Brighouse party was fed at Bridge End Sunday School before moving into temporary sleeping quarters. Now was the time for an appeal to people's generosity, even sense of duty, in asking them to welcome strangers. There had been no pre-evacuation surveys of possible billets, as in the reception areas, and there is evidence to show that nationally the first flush of enthusiasm for taking in evacuees had worn off, even by 1940. After all, 'welcoming strangers' into one's house, for an indefinite period, is something that most people would prefer not to do. Unease, even fear, are natural responses to such a suggestion.

> *Local billeting officers could resort to the law and enforce compulsion on householders to take in evacuees. By the Civil Defence Act of 1939, a refusal incurred a £50 fine or three months in prison. They were, however, reluctant to implement compulsion, relying on the voluntary principle wherever possible.*

Despite the difficulties presented in looking for accommodation for family groups, by the end of the first week 250 of the 400 Halifax arrivals had been found homes. An alternative to placing the refugees with residents was to find vacant houses for families, and the people of Halifax set to with a will to provide bedding and furniture. The Edwards family thus found a home in Sunnybank, Ovenden. To provide continued support, a Guernsey Club was formed in September 1940. A later expression of local goodwill was the formation of the Halifax Channel Island Committee, with its aim of, "Visiting, supervision and assistance of Channel Island evacuees in Halifax."

This group of refugees could not return home as the fancy took them, for the Channel Islands remained in the vice-like grip of the Germans until the end of the war. Therefore they became part of the fabric of local life, so much so that not all of them returned to those seemingly sunny and attractive islands after the war. Colin Wakefield of Lee Mount worked alongside some of them at the Yorkshire Electricity Board in the post-war years. Joan Sutcliffe saw a number of evacuees from Guernsey come to work at Asquith's. She forged friendships with some of them, which took her on frequent visits to Guernsey after the war, links that are maintained to this day. Basil Cavinet had only been 12 years old when caught up in that frantic exit from Guernsey in 1940. He then spent five years with his family at Brookfoot, Brighouse, years during which he was, "overwhelmed by the friendship and hospitality." The Brighouse Channel Islands Society expressed its gratitude at the end of the war by presenting an illuminated scroll which hangs in the Smith Gallery, Brighouse, today. Evacuation may have been a painful necessity of the time, but new and enduring friendships, even marriages, were amongst its more positive legacies.

The reception areas had structures in place for the absorption of masses of evacuees, and as heavy bombing began in 1940, they were called into play once again. The Hebden Royd records for these years, in the Archives section

A tribute to Brighouse from Channel Island evacuees.
Courtesy of Calderdale MBC Libraries, Museums and Arts

of Halifax Central Library, are remarkably complete. They provide a fascinating picture of local officials grappling with unprecedented problems for which past experience had provided no guidance. In the summer of 1940, when it had become clear that the 'phoney war' was over, a circular to 2,800 householders across the Hebden Royd and Hepton Rural districts had produced a disheartening response. The circular had asked for volunteers to accept evacuees. Only 37 had expressed willingness, and a massive 2,741 had not even made a reply. Officials felt, however, that attitudes would change if heavy bombing began.

Later, in September, the Hebden Royd Evacuation Committee received notification that the area would be receiving some 500 evacuees in October 1940, refugees from the

---

"the lot of a reception area official was not a happy one"

London 'blitz.' In a letter with more than a hint of weary resignation about it, the Clerk to the Hebden Royd Urban District Council, Mr Raymond Ashworth, demonstrated that the lot of a reception area official was not a happy one. The letter was addressed to the Regional Evacuation Officer at Leeds, and whilst Mr Ashworth said that, of course, the council would do its duty, he had to point out the following. Three weeks earlier, 300 soldiers had arrived in Hebden Bridge and had occupied an empty clothing factory, Brown's Mill. At weekends, wives and families often arrived on visits, sometimes looking for overnight stays. To make the accommodation problem worse,

unofficial or 'private' evacuees were entering the district from Newcastle, Manchester, Liverpool, London and the Channel Islands.

Nevertheless, the first batch of new evacuees arrived at Hebden Bridge station on October 23rd 1940 – 88 in total. Three more batches arrived in November. The projected total of 500 was not reached, but there were more arrivals in February and March 1941. London was not the only source for these official evacuations. In June 1941, over 100 children, mothers and helpers entered the district from Brighton, and at this point it was stated that there were between 1,100 and 1,200 evacuees in the area, with the prospect of more to come.

Billeting was now a real problem for the local Evacuation Committee, especially in view of the dispiriting returns to the circular of summer 1940, asking for volunteers. Matters were not helped by the flow of unofficial evacuees, although a private body had set itself up to try and cater for their needs – the Hebden Royd Refugee Relief Committee.

It had brought in 41 evacuees by the end of January 1941 and at this point the Council's Evacuation Committee took over the responsibility for them.

Spreading a little happiness – the WVS distributing toys to local evacuees.

Courtesy of Stephen Gee

In October 1940, the Hebden Royd Refugee Relief Committee had welcomed three families from London – 20 people in all – and accommodated them in three cottages at Brearley, having scratched around to find furniture for them. All of them had faced the terrors of the 'blitz' and reportedly loved the scenery and peace of the Calder Valley. The children fitted the stereotypical image of evacuee kids from the city, describing cows as "horses with horns on."

One way or another, unaccompanied children from this second major evacuation were billeted in private homes throughout the Hebden Royd and Hepton Rural districts. With varying degrees of willingness, evacuee children were accepted without the need for compulsion. So far so good, but a household was only informed as to the number of children it was liable to take. The process of distributing the children was, in some cases, rather more ramshackle. Sometimes they were simply assembled in a local centre and adults came and made their choice - rather like a cattle market.

A solution to the problem of accommodating families was found in the requisitioning of vacant property. Unfortunately, much of the property was vacant for a reason – that it was condemned and due for demolition – but evacuee families often preferred this option to that of splitting up families. Bankfoot Terrace, High Street and New Street (the latter two now long demolished) were just some of the areas of Hebden Bridge where vacant property was requisitioned. Brook Street, in Todmorden, was used for the same purpose. Evacuee families from London were also to be found in Halifax in 1944. Geoff Whiteley lived on the Bracewell Estate, Wheatley, and in a block of six houses, the Whiteleys had five evacuee families for company.

Every evacuee had a story to tell, one that would be passed down as part of the family's history, sometimes attaining legendary proportions. In June 1941 the Riches family, true Cockneys from Bethnal Green, had made the long journey north to Leeds by train. From

there, the destination was Mytholmroyd, and as they approached it by bus they tried to wrap their cockney tongues around this strange name. Nan Riches, accompanied by her young children, Shirley and Ronnie, as well as her teenage brother and sister, had one consoling thought. She had been told that the family had been allocated a house in Pall Mall, which evoked dreams of tree-lined West End boulevards.

As it turned out, Pall Mall was a row of derelict property awaiting demolition, situated in Mytholmroyd on what is now the car park adjoining the White Lion. This had none of the idyllic qualities of Stan Pierce's Hardcastle Crags paradise, but then Nan Riches did not want to be on the hills. Practical considerations carried more weight, such as nearness of shops and buses. The family revelled in the safety and tranquillity of their surroundings, but one 'thing' was missing – dad. George Riches had

George and Shirley Riches – from Bethnal Green to Mytholmroyd.

gone to France with the British Expeditionary Force; had been evacuated from St Nazaire in 1940 on the troopship, 'Lancastria;' had been miraculously rescued after a German bomb had blown it apart; and had last been heard of in Icelandic waters.

Now the story took on the strangest twist of all. George had returned to England, but in the turmoil of evacuation had lost touch with his family. He only knew that his wife was in a place called Mytholmroyd, somewhere in Yorkshire. Fate took a hand, and George was posted to Halifax, still unaware of how close he really was to his family. One afternoon, emerging from the King's Head at King Cross, he saw a bus waiting at the stop. A casual remark from a passer-by told him that it was going to Mytholmroyd, and George hopped on. Around 20 minutes later, he was knocking at the door at Pall Mall and the rest, as they say, is history.

George and Nan Riches fully intended to return to Bethnal Green. In fact, "When we go

That was one end of the evacuee spectrum. At the other end was the fleeting emergency visit. Jean Fields, for example, living at Pellon Lane, came down for breakfast one morning to find around 20 people sleeping on the floor. They were all relatives from Liverpool who had been bombed out. The unique conditions of wartime made people more readily able to accept such unexpected upheavals. Jean's mother, apparently unperturbed, catered for them all until they could return a few days later. She made bread in a huge baking bowl and only became flustered when one of the young children fell right into it, "Just as the dough was rising!"

Most of the evacuees and refugees fell somewhere between the permanence of the

Evacuee party at Mytholmroyd – Nan Riches in the middle of the back row, holding daughter Jacqui.

back...," was their constant refrain. In the end they stayed, moving into a council house on the new Banksfield Estate at the end of the war. With a family that had grown to five children by 1946, and their gregarious natures, they soon became part of the local community, even though they remained 'off-comed `uns.'

Riches and the transience of the bombed out Liverpudlians. Movement and change was a recurring theme as evacuee families tended to return home once an immediate threat was over, only to pack up and leave again at the next danger.

LIVING WITH STRANGERS

"We need to create a better understanding between the people of the North and those who have come from the South." Lady Allerton, May 1941

Welcoming strangers is relatively simple; living with strangers poses more problems. The migration of thousands of city dwellers (usually from the poorest areas) into more rural areas was bound to produce a degree of culture shock – on both sides. 'Horror stories' about evacuee

---

" it was widely held that evacuee children were highly resistant to bathing"

---

children soon began to circulate. A kind of 'Richter' scale of outrage began with bedwetting at the bottom, lice infestation and swearing somewhere in the middle, culminating in a peak of indignation at thieving and absence of toilet training. Not only this, it was widely held that evacuee children were highly resistant to bathing and were sometimes sewn into their clothes for winter.

The 1939 evacuees from Bradford had given the Calderdale reception areas a little taster of what was to come, but the incomers were probably not unlike the local children and had not stayed very long. The years 1940 and 1941, however, presented a very different scenario. Hundreds of children arrived, mainly from London and predominantly from poor, working class districts. The roll call of names – Bethnal Green, Dagenham, Charlton, Greenwich – sounded strange to most local people, particularly when expressed in a 'funny' accent. To some upon whom these children were billeted, not only was their speech strange, but their behaviour was too. Halifax and Calderdale can produce its fair share of evacuee 'horror stories,' but in common with the rest of the country, the picture is liable to exaggeration and distortion.

Bedwetting was a very common problem, but it is easy to forget the anxiety of children

who had been wrenched out of a familiar situation and placed among strangers. Vincent Holt's parents, in Todmorden, received two young evacuee boys from Dagenham in 1940. They were utterly alienated from their new surroundings and so distressed at being separated from their parents that they cried themselves to sleep every night. The first visit from their mother resulted in a swift return to Dagenham. Some children not only had the pain of separation, but were also traumatised by their experiences of the 'blitz.' One girl from Edinburgh tended to startle her classmates at Lumbutts School, Todmorden, by screaming and throwing herself under the desk every time an aeroplane passed overhead. Strange behaviour, yes, but not inexplicable.

The 'collision of worlds' was most marked where working class children were billeted on middle class households. A Todmorden couple, with a four year old evacuee from Dagenham,

A WVS leaflet on how to avoid evacuee 'culture shock.'

Courtesy of Calderdale MBC Libraries, Museums and Arts

were taken aback that she had no concept of walks and picnics at the weekends. The usual routine at home for her was to play outside the pub whilst her parents enjoyed themselves inside. Other local hosts complained that evacuees constantly demanded fish and chips, and some of them related tales of heads that were absolutely alive with lice. True enough, no doubt, but the tellers of such tales need not have travelled far from home to find local children with the same tastes and ailments.

Where evacuees ended up in those working class households which had room for them, the complaints were likely to be economic. The billeting rates for 1940 were widely felt to be inadequate – 10s 6d (52.5p) per week for a child over 14, and 8s 6d (42.5p) for a child below that age. This was for basic 'keep,' but some people grumbled that they had to re-clothe evacuees, with no help from their parents. The latter occasionally came to stay – another extra cost. A handful of hosts found that they simply could not cope. The Evacuation Committee at Hebden Royd on one occasion received an impassioned letter from a Mytholmroyd couple. Their evacuee boy was, "running wild" – playing truant, straying onto the railway embankment, falling into the Elphin Brook, constantly needing attention for cuts and bruises. Both the man and his wife worked long hours on war contracts. They felt that they were not in a position to care for the boy, and entreated the Committee to remove him.

This the Committee did, and they placed the boy in Heath House, in Hebden Bridge. From the very first it had been understood that there would be 'problem' or 'difficult' children who could not

easily be accommodated in the billeting system. Heath House was a hostel for such children, owned by the Council, and set up in 1940. It had room for 17, but it was never intended as a permanent base. Wherever possible, Heath House was used as a temporary solution until problems had been ironed out and a suitable new billet had been found. The hostel had a full time matron, and the children attended the local school at Mytholm, with a full programme of activities for their spare

A HEALTHY CHILD IS A HAPPY CHILD

A REGULAR ROUTINE is the basis of a healthy child's day. Waking, meal and bed-times should vary as little as possible.

A young child requires eleven–twelve hours' sleep each night and a rest during the day.

PREVENTION IS BETTER THAN CURE

The following rules will go far to prevent the Minor Maladies of childhood ; and to lighten the burden of caring for the children.

1. **RIGHT FEEDING.** For health, a varied and well-balanced diet, with plenty of fresh vegetables and fluids, is necessary and is the best safeguard against colds and constipation. (These two complaints themselves often lead to many other ailments.) All milk should be boiled or pasteurised.

2. **CLEANLINESS.**

   (a) **Baths.** Frequent baths are advisable. If there should be a water-shortage, it would be better for each child to have an enamel basin of fresh water for sponging, than to share a bath. When the children are stripped for their baths be on the watch for spots, sore places or blistered heels. Taken in time these may give little trouble.

   (b) **Teeth.** Tooth-brushes should be kept separate and clean. Where tooth-brushes cannot be provided, give a piece of raw apple or carrot after each meal, and a drink of water at bed-time.

   (c) **Nails** carry infection—therefore, keep them short and clean.

   (d) **Care of Head.** Children may have been subjected to infection on the journey. Heads should be combed with a small tooth-comb for three days. All heads should be washed weekly and inspected daily. Report dirty heads to the Health Visitor or District Nurs at once.

   (e) **Clothing.** Regular changes of underclothes are important for cleanliness and health. Be sure the children do not sleep in any garment they have worn all day.

3. **VENTILATION.** A window should be open at night. Remember that children require relatively more air space than adults.

   Let the children have separate beds where possible. If sharing, put bolster between them or let them sleep head to foot

Sound advice for keeping your evacuee healthy.

Courtesy of Calderdale MBC Libraries, Museums and Arts

time. Hepton Rural Council had a hostel for boys at Slater Ing, and within its area fell the Burnside Hostel. This acted as a 33-bed hospital for all the evacuee children from the immediate locality, and also from Sowerby Bridge and Ripponden. Clearly a high degree of organisation was required within the reception area to cater for this new community within a community.

If host families sometimes had complaints, so did evacuees, although it has to be admitted that the one made by Mrs Brand was rather a strange one. Along with her sons, 'Harry Boy' and 'Charlie Boy,' she was billeted with Mrs Doreen Russell's family at Siddal. It wasn't long before they all departed back to London because they could not abide the quietness of Siddal life. Rather more serious was the complaint of an evacuee lady with a young child billeted with a family at Mytholmroyd.

Not only were they ostracised, but were denied access to lighting and cooking facilities, this in the middle of January 1941. A stern letter from the Evacuation Committee's tribunal soon put matters to rights.

In the middle of what must sometimes have seemed like a battleground stood the Women's

---

"The members of the WVS ranked among the heroines of the Home Front".

Voluntary Service, attempting to ease problems on all sides. The members of the WVS ranked among the heroines of the Home Front. From the outbreak of war, they answered every call, and amidst all this work the stress was on the word 'voluntary.' Out of one million members of the WVS in 1941, only around 200 were full-time and paid. With the trial run of Dunkirk behind them, the WVS were ideally fitted to the work of receiving, settling and monitoring evacuees. Two members of the WVS served on the Hebden Royd Evacuation Committee, and they were soon involved in collecting bedding and furniture for the families in requisitioned houses. A clothing depot was set up on Market Street. By May 1941, the WVS had transformed Ashley House, in Hebden Bridge, into a rest and recreational centre for local evacuee mothers and children, with a nursery, a rest room, and offices for the WVS and the Billeting Officer. Interestingly, in her speech at the opening of Ashley House, Lady Allerton, County Organiser of the WVS, said that she hoped, "Such a place would help to create a better understanding between the people of the North and those who had come from the South."

If Lady Allerton was using diplomatic language about the 'collision of worlds,' then it was

---

ADVICE ON SOME POSSIBLE DIFFICULTIES

Remember that the younger children especially will be feeling home-sick, frightened and thoroughly upset and over-excited for several days.

They may refuse their food for a time. Do not force them to eat : but on the other hand do not offer alternatives.

Because of the strain and tension, some of the children may have bad habits, such as bed wetting. Do not scold or punish them. This will only prolong the difficulty. Try getting them up at about 10 p.m. ; give extra warmth—an additional blanket. Should this difficulty persist, seek advice from the District Nurse.

A supply of material for mackintosh overlays for the beds of young children has been ordered by the Government and will be issued to householders by local authorities.

Be patient ! Give them as much affection and sense of security as possible. Do all you can to gain their confidence. A sense of security will be given by a regular life. See that they have plenty of occupation and play. Discuss nothing in front of the children that has frightened them or may frighten them in the future. Do not discuss the child's health or conduct in its presence.

Cuts, bruises and falls are inevitable. Burns and scalds are fortunately rare ; but you should have a few simple remedies in the house for all such mishaps.

For cuts, an ointment such as Iodine-medol is good, and does not sting. Failing the ointment use Iodine or Friar's Balsam.

Sore places should be reported at once. Meanwhile, apply zinc ointment.

The WVS was well aware of the problems of evacuees.
Courtesy of Calderdale MBC Libraries, Museums and Arts

felt in a more literal sense in the rough and tumble of school playgrounds. Here suspicious locals and defensive evacuees put each other to the test. On his first day at St Chad's School at Hove Edge, Brighouse, evacuee Peter Cobbold was advanced upon by a boy who greeted him with the words, "You from London? I'm gonna bray thee." Peter did not quite understand the language, but the intention was plain enough and so he got his retaliation in first. Such battles were fought out the length and breadth of Halifax and Calderdale, but once locals and evacuees had tried each other out, they tended to accept each other for what they were, perhaps more so than their parents.

At Stubbings School, Hebden Bridge, there was a whole class of evacuees, complete with their own teacher. Keith Newbitt became firm friends with one of them, Roy Cutler, and was vastly entertained by the antics of another of

them, John Garrod. This ebullient character was publicly caned for pinning Barry Lomas' ear to the door with a dart. Through such cavalier behaviour he endeared himself to the whole school, locals and evacuees alike, with the possible exception of Barry.

Colin Wakefield's mother, Doris, helped to set up a reception centre for evacuees at Lee Mount Baptist Church, Halifax. The Sunday School was equipped with beds and cooking equipment, and Doris might be called on at any time, day or night, to help provide some temporary accommodation prior to billeting. Any overspill evacuees invariably ended up in the Wakefield house for a night or two, and Colin's education was broadened by his meeting people from various parts of England and Europe.

The 'horror stories' arising from the 1940-41 evacuation wave were just one side of the coin. A mass migration of people is bound to create social tensions, but for every negative story a positive one, imbued with friendship and kindness, can be unearthed. John Tolley, in Hebden Bridge, cannot have been too happy about sharing his bed for a time with a London evacuee, Tony Bulman. However, the Bulman family soon found its own accommodation, and after the war the Tolleys were invited to have a holiday in Greenwich – a return of favours. Dora Longbottom, living at Copley, volunteered to have an evacuee from Acton, London. She did not have the luck of the draw in that the five year old had a caliper on one leg and an iron platform under the other foot. He presented special problems, but she did her best for him whilst operating on a financial 'shoestring.'

Some local foster parents simply took on evacuees as their own children, giving them equal love and attention. The same Peter Cobbold who had to stand his corner in St Chad's schoolyard, spent many happy months with Tom and Edith Mason and their son, David, at Halifax Road, Brighouse. To Peter, the caring couple were simply his new auntie

Mrs Newbitt with Keith, who witnessed the Stubbings dart throwing incident.

and uncle. The story of one Illingworth lady can only be called inspiring. Although she had two boys of her own, she accepted a mentally handicapped evacuee. He could neither use cutlery nor even fasten a button. She lavished patient attention on him, eventually teaching him how to use a spoon – a process which took seven months. She made a waistcoat for him, with an extra big button and hole, on which he could practise. By the time the evacuee left this extraordinary lady, he could virtually dress himself, although shoelaces still defeated him.

By 1942, the worst of the bombing was over, so much so that the official evacuation programme was suspended in the September of that year. Things seemed to have stabilised in Britain, and in spite of cautionary advice from officials, many children had returned home. The Hebden Royd Evacuation Committee, reporting in March 1944, stated that out of 1,328 evacuees received since the war began, only 305 remained. Of these, 230 were family groups living in 44 requisitioned houses. With the Allied invasion of Normandy taking place in June 1944, and talk in some quarters of the war being over by Christmas, all seemed set fair.

Then, literally out of the blue, the 'doodlebugs' began to fall. On June 13th 1944

"the new threat precipitated the third great evacuation wave."

---

the first V1, or flying bomb, fell on London. This was followed by many more, at all times of night and day, and the new threat precipitated the third great evacuation wave. Unofficial evacuees began to enter Halifax and Calderdale almost immediately, many of them returnees from previous evacuations. The first official group arrived at Halifax railway station over the weekend of 8th and 9th July, around 800 unaccompanied children. Halifax was well prepared this time, and the youngsters were whisked away to eight rest centres manned by the WVS. Private billets were urgently required, however, and the Mayor, Councillor

T. Greenwood, urged the people of Halifax to, "Regard such a service as a thank-offering for their own safety and well-being." Somehow the task was achieved, and with numbers never before experienced by Halifax. The thankless task of being Chief Billeting Officer had fallen to Mr J.W. Beaumont, although he did get his thanks in October 1944, when the Town Council congratulated him on the, "successful billeting of some thousands of evacuees from London and the south of England."

Among the more pro-active of the citizens of Halifax had been the Music mistress at the Princess Mary High School, Miss Webster. A personal friend of the headmistress of Streatham Hill High, in the heart of London, she had heard at first hand of the terrors being faced daily by the girls studying there. It did not take long for Miss Webster to persuade the parents of the Princess Mary girls to provided safe havens for the Streatham Hill students. Not only this, the Halifax girls and their London guests would be able to work together at school. It was in such ways as this that the upheavals of war created unique opportunities for relationships that otherwise would never have come into being.

As a 13 year old at the Princess Mary High School, Jennifer Wade, an only child, viewed the prospect of a companion of the same age with great excitement. She was not to be disappointed when Jeanette Mandler arrived from London, a girl with a touch of metropolitan sophistication about her. Jennifer and Jeanette 'hit it off' immediately and became good friends. The bond survives today, even though Jeanette lives in Boston, Massachusetts and Jennifer Wade has become Jennifer Pell, the busy owner of Fred Wade's bookshop in Halifax. The two friends keep in touch, visit each other and are godmothers to each other's daughters.

On the same weekend as around 800 unaccompanied children arrived at Halifax railway station, about 200 were received at Brighouse, and had been billeted by noon on Monday. Another batch fetched up at Sowerby Bridge, and others proceeded into the Upper Calder Valley. The Hebden Royd Evacuation

A lifetime of friendship – Jennifer Pell (left) and Jeanette Fullerton (right).

> *Only one prosecution was proposed in Hebden Royd for a refusal to take an evacuee. This was dropped in November 1944 when the Mytholmroyd householder in question relented.*

Pauline and Geoffrey Geier, evacuated from Chiswick in London, were caught up in those hectic summer months of 1944. Their story illustrates the planning and goodwill of the Hebden Royd Evacuation Committee, but also the pressures that perhaps led to breakdowns in communication. Pauline, aged eight, had expected to be billeted with her five year old brother, Geoffrey. The planning was good in that there was no 'cattle market' aspect to it. The evacuees had been designated homes already. On the other hand, neither Geoffrey nor Pauline was informed as to where the other one was. One week later, whilst playing outside her host home in Hebden Bridge, 5 Eaves Mount, Pauline bumped into Geoffrey. He had been billeted at 7 Eaves Mount!

This was not the best of starts, but both of them were happy in their new surroundings. Pauline stayed with the Scarborough family, and as there were three daughters there – Agnes, Joyce and Mary – she had plenty of playmates. Geoffrey stayed with two elderly sisters, Lily and Ethel Greenwood. Both

Committee had been warning of the impending influx and was deeply concerned. Unofficial evacuees were already arriving in some numbers. There was no alternative to compulsory billeting, especially as WVS rest and recreation centres were already being used as temporary accommodation. A hastily jotted down note in the Calderdale Archives records what must have been a horrifying prospect for the beleaguered clerk to the Hebden Royd Council, Mr Raymond Ashworth. The note suggested that Hebden Royd should expect a total of 1,855 evacuees by August 5th 1944. In the event, far fewer arrived.

55 years on – evacuee Pauline White (formerly Geier) sits between Agnes (left) and Joyce (right) of the Scarborough family.

Pauline and Geoffrey were treated with great kindness, and Pauline's wonderment at the breathtaking scenery caused her to think for a time that maybe she, "had died and gone to heaven." As for Geoffrey, he was content to scramble about the slopes and through the woods with a freedom and sense of security he had never felt in bomb-shattered London. Pauline and Geoffrey returned to Chiswick in 1945, and lost touch with their new friends. However, there was a pleasant postscript when, through the power of the Internet, a joyous reunion took place in 2000. Pauline met up with two of the former Scarborough sisters, and 'burned the midnight oil' as they caught up on 55 years.

It would be naïve to think, however, that all was sweetness and light with regard to the Upper Calder Valley and its evacuees in 1944. A letter of complaint, signed by 32 people, was sent to the Hebden Royd Council in August 1944. It spoke on behalf of the private rental sector, and accused the Evacuation Committee of high-handedness in requisitioning property that was only temporarily vacant due to a change in tenancy. As an afterthought, the letter added that the area had too many evacuees anyway!

If some of the local landlords were not happy, a number of evacuee children were none too thrilled either. No sooner had one boy arrived, in July 1944, than he 'voted with his feet.' He managed to get himself from Heptonstall to Halifax station, where he tendered up two shillings at the booking office and asked for a ticket to London. The police were called and he was duly returned to his host family. Heptonstall seems to have had an unsettling effect on some evacuees. Four girls billeted there also set off for their London homes, via Halifax, and two Sowerby Bridge evacuees joined them in their escape bid. Again the police had to do their duty. It was reported that some of the children from London who arrived at Halifax in early July were soon out in the fields helping local farmers. However, whereas some children enjoyed the fresh air, beauty and tranquillity of the countryside, others clearly found rural life unbearably dull.

> *In December 1944, five evacuee children appeared in a local juvenile court for, "cruelly ill-treating a cow"- at Heptonstall. The boys had chased it with sticks until it fell over a wall, broke a leg and had to be destroyed. The boys were from the Slater Ing Hostel and were most repentant. Whilst not defending their behaviour, a Ministry official regretted the lack of facilities for children, "to let off steam."*

Standing somewhere between discontented locals and unhappy evacuees stood the hard working and severely tried welfare officers, attempting to placate both sides. They found themselves truly 'between a rock and a hard place.' The Sanderson sisters, Eleanor and Hilda Mary, became almost legendary for their unremitting toil on behalf of evacuees in Mytholmroyd. The Riches family described them as the "guardian angels" of all those in need. Nevertheless, the work took its toll, and in 1944 one of them had to resign due to a breakdown of health. Her letter to the Evacuation Committee explaining her reasons, gives a revealing and moving insight into the everyday trials of a welfare officer. Hilda Mary

"reduced her to a state of mental and physical exhaustion."

Sanderson, a WVS member strongly motivated by a sense of Christian duty, felt that she had achieved much. However, the constant labour and squabbles (sometimes between evacuee families themselves), and the tendency of the River Calder to sometimes flood evacuee homes, had reduced her to a state of mental and physical exhaustion.

The highs and lows of the evacuee experience, for residents and refugees alike, were repeated right across Calderdale and in Halifax itself. If tension was a recurring theme, then harmony could also be created in the most unpromising of circumstances. The story of the Goldthorpe family, of Holmfield, shows how evacuation could bring out the best in people rather than the worst. One evening in 1944, with the flying bombs terrorising London, a train containing a party of evacuees pulled in to Holmfield station. They were escorted to the reception centre – the Sunday School on Shay Lane. Among them was Verena Hurren, from North London, with her twin ten week old daughters, Geraldine and Dixie. Verena's sister, Esther, and her 18 month old son Peter completed an extended family of five.

The Goldthorpes had a fairly spacious four bedroomed terraced house, next to the Holmfield Co-op, but it already had eight occupants – themselves, their five children and an uncle. Betty was not the sort of person to be daunted by the task of sorting out sleeping arrangements and catering for a mere thirteen people. A dash of sound common sense helped, but above all it was her generosity of spirit that enabled her to take everything in her stride. It was always 'open house' at the Goldthorpes. The focal point of the week was Sunday lunch, when everyone sat around a huge scrubbed table in the kitchen. 'Everyone' included Betty's family, her new evacuee family and any friends who happened to drop in.

Verena's sister and her son stayed about six months, but Verena and her twins stayed for a year. In that time, many members of Verena's large family descended on the Goldthorpes for varying periods of time, including her mother, mother-in-law

Evacuee Verena Hurren with twins Geraldine and Dixie.

In the next few days the Sunday school slowly emptied as billets were found, but Verena's extended family was determined to stay together and after a week nowhere had been found for them. It was at this point that George Goldthorpe stepped into their lives. He was both a foreman at Whitaker's Brewery and a part-time caretaker at Holmfield Sunday School. Informing his wife, Betty, of the plight of Verena's family, she had no hesitation in saying, "Then we must take them in."

The indomitable Betty Goldthorpe (centre) surrounded by family and extended family.

and four sisters with assorted offspring. It was always the same with Betty – a warm and good-humoured welcome; no fuss. As Verena was to say later, "If ever hearts and a house were elastic – then the Goldthorpes of Shay Lane qualified."

> *In her happy year at Holmfield, Verena was initiated into some of the niceties of Yorkshire life, such as buying 'spice' with her sweet coupons; eating fish cakes from the chip shop (never experienced since); and tea always served in pint pots.*

After Verena took her leave, in 1945, the two families did not just stay in touch. They had become a part of each other's lives. Verena was able to return hospitality after the war, when Betty's parents made an overnight stay in London 'en route' to visit a grandson in South Africa. George, Uncle Albert and friends stayed with Verena on trips to Wembley for Rugby League Cup Finals. When one of Verena's twins was married, in 1964, first on the guest list was Mrs Betty Goldthorpe. Betty died in 1997, aged 93, but the mutual family bond continues. Betty's daughter, Brenda Gaukroger still corresponds with Verena, now in Ely, Cambridgeshire. Hitler's 'vengeance' weapons did much to destroy families, but by one of the strange paradoxes of war, the V1s brought together these two families, enriching and enhancing the lives of both of them.

The route south that Verena and her twins took in 1945 was one that was followed by many others. The last V1 flying bomb fell on March 1st 1945. From September 1944, however, they had been superseded by an even greater menace – the V2 rockets. The last one of these fell on 27th March, after which the Allied armies overran the last of their launching sites. Thoughts were now beginning to turn to home – this time for good.

London was not yet safe by February 1945, but an official party of evacuees returned to Brighton from Hebden Royd in that month. The return gathered impetus after 'Victory in

Guernsey Club members celebrating 'VE Day' in May 1945, in Halifax. Florence and Nora Edwards, with Jeane and Peter in front, form the group on the left.

Europe Day,' 8th May, and more than one trainload of evacuees left Halifax for London in June, containing evacuees from right across Calderdale. However, if the arrival of evacuees in the district had not been a simple matter, neither in some cases was their return. What if some did not want to go back? What if some had no home to go back to? These, and other knotty problems, were now what local officials had to turn their minds to.

Once again, the Hebden Royd records present at least a part of the picture. The return of evacuee children to Brighton in February had thrown up unexpected issues. Three children could not be returned, and had to be retained in Hebden Royd. Sadly, in one case, the parents could not be traced. Sadder still, the other two were not allowed to go back because home conditions were deemed to be unsatisfactory. Their natural parents were either incapable of looking after them, or were unwilling to have them back.

With regard to evacuee families, the problems generally revolved around housing. A letter had been sent from the Council, early in 1945, asking the families whether they intended to return to their former homes or to stay in the Hebden Royd or Hepton areas. Those who chose the latter course usually did so because they had been bombed out or had abandoned a low quality home. Many were from London, but there were also families from Brighton, Bristol, Liverpool, Manchester and North Shields. The overall total of parents and children wishing to remain at the end of July 1945 was 135, although a few may have come back to the area after this.

Those who stayed were, because of their circumstances, high on the list for the new council houses that were being built. This may not have gone down well with the locals but all of the evacuee families lived in houses that were earmarked for slum clearance or had been

"not willing to accept the evacuees as tenants."

requisitioned from the private rental market. The time had now come for de-requisitioning, but in a letter from the Council to the Regional Evacuation Officer at Leeds, it was stated that almost all the landlords, "are not willing to accept the evacuees as tenants."

If this sounds somewhat uncharitable, then it was reinforced by a letter to the Hebden Royd Council from an evacuee. He wanted to stay and apply for a council house, but he wondered how long evacuees would continue to be treated, "as people at a lower level." Lack of charity on the part of some was counterbalanced by the more generous natures of others. The two Brighton boys who were not allowed to return to unfit homes were adopted locally, and were given more care and love by their adoptive parents than they had ever received, or were likely to have received, from their natural parents.

The sharper edges of tension between locals and evacuees gradually began to be smoothed away with the passage of years, but it was the children of the evacuees who fully blended into local communities and became 'locals' themselves. If this was true for Hebden Royd, then it was likely to have been equally true for Calderdale, Halifax and the country at large. The evacuees changed the social landscape forever.

THE INVISIBLE ENEMY

Hitler will give no warning – so always carry your gas mask.'
Government poster, 1939

The Ordnance Survey Map on the two following pages was produced by the German General Staff of the Army Division for War Maps. It was a special edition for military use only. This section shows Central Halifax, but the map extended to cover Ovenden, Northowram, and Hipperholme. The map pinpoints factories, a power station, the railway goods yard, railway bridges, waterworks and reservoirs. It is likely to have been made in the early stages of the Second World War and as it was commissioned for military purposes, the features especially marked out were probably targets for potential bombing raids. Parachutists could also have benefited, but that is less likely to have been the purpose of the map.

The information it provided may well have persuaded German High Command that Halifax was a 'textiles town,' and that there were more important industrial targets quite close at hand, such as Manchester and Sheffield. This offers one explanation as to why Halifax escaped relatively unscathed from bombing during the war, but it also assumes that the Germans remained unaware that, for example, air and sea torpedoes were being made at the Dean Clough complex, or that engineering firms such as Firth Brown from Sheffield and Armstrong-Siddely from Birmingham had moved in there.

In 1939, however, all this lay ahead and Halifax and its surrounding districts had to prepare for the possibility of a full-scale air offensive. At first, the great preoccupation and

---

"Chlorine, Phosgene and Picric were all regarded as lethal,"

---

fear was gas. As early as 1937, the Home Office had published a booklet entitled 'Personal Protection Against Gas.' In July 1939, four Civil Defence pamphlets were sent to every household in the country and the use of gas masks was a prominent theme in two of them. Those who were expected to deal with a gas attack, the police and air raid precaution personnel, were sent classified information about types of gases, how to detect them and how to treat victims. Gas was no simple business. Chlorine, Phosgene and Picric were all regarded as lethal, whereas Mustard Gas tended merely to disable. Another group of gases was intended to have a hallucinatory effect, inducing mass panic. Decontamination was a major issue and the advice disseminated ranged from boiling clothes in 2 oz of washing soda for between 30 to 60 minutes, to decontaminating house walls and roofs. Even roads and gardens would have to go through the procedure, at a rate of 12 lbs of bleach per square yard.

At a local level, the Halifax Air Raid Precaution Committee was in existence by 1937, and an anti-gas training centre at Stoney Royd was in use by March 1938. Woodside Baths, at Boothtown, had a decontamination area installed. Decontamination Centres were also set up around the district. Hebden Bridge had one at King Street. The no less sinister name of Cleansing Stations were applied to some of them, for example the one at Brighouse, in the Corporation Storeyard on Clifton Street, and the one at Sowerby Bridge, at the junction of Station and Norland Roads.

A simple device existed for the detection of gas in the air, for gas bombs could fall from the skies without the noise of high explosives. Both John Tolley at Hebden Bridge and Philip Hanson at Pellon saw this device on the ground. In Philip's case it stood outside the local air raid warden's house, and had the appearance of a short bird table – a post with a two feet square platform on top. The square was painted yellowish-green, but would change colour if gas appeared in the air. Were this ever to happen, the warden's duty was clear – to race around his area using a hand rattle to signal a gas alert. The use of a hand bell would announce the later 'all-clear.'

A German military map pinpointing Halifax targets.

Einzelobjekte

48 **Textilfabrik**

50 **Elektrizitätswerk**

Eisenbahnwerkstätten, Bahnhofsanlagen

Dampfelektrizitätswerk

Eisenindustrie

Maschinenfabrik

Wasserwerk (Erdbehälter)

Nagelfabrik, Drahtfabrik

Textilindustrie

Kläranlage, Abwässerwerk

Ziegelei

Fabrikanlage unbekannter Art

Eisenbahnbrücke

Straßenbrücke

Tunnel

Courtesy of Calderdale MBC Libraries, Museums and Arts

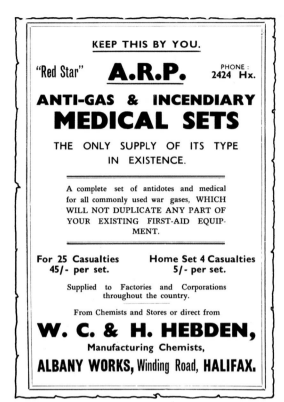

A worrying sign of the times.

The following little ditty was widely circulated as an educational device, but may well only have increased confusion.

If you get a choking feeling, and a smell of musty hay,
You can bet your bottom dollar there is Phosgene on the way;
But the smell of Bleaching Powder will inevitably mean,
That the enemy you're meeting is the gas we call Chlorine.

If your skin begins a-twitching, and for tears you cannot see,
It isn't mother peeling onions, but a dose of CAP.
If the smell resembles Peardrops, then you'd better not delay-
It isn't father sucking sweets, but the blinking KSK.

If you get a pungent odour as you're going home to tea,
You can safely make a guess that they're using BBC.
And lastly, while geraniums look pleasant in a bed,
Beware the smell in war-time: if it's Lewisite, you're dead!

The public, understandably, was reluctant to face up to these prospective horrors. The distribution of millions of gas masks, and mass fittings of these throughout the country, persuaded people to take matters more seriously. 'Hitler will give no warning – so always carry your gas mask,' proclaimed an official poster of 1939, and at first this was faithfully obeyed. Children presented a particular problem, mainly because gas masks were so repulsive in appearance and so uncomfortable to wear. It was quite an inspired notion to fashion the 'Mickey Mouse' masks for very young children and by January 1940 two million of these were in circulation. As a pupil of St Mary's School, Mill Bank, Hazel Cartwright was able to experience at first hand the ways in which children can respond to a new and strange situation – sometimes with

" had to be carried from the classroom struggling and screaming"

horror, often with humour, and always with an eye to manipulating it to their own advantage.

On the first day of 'official' gas mask practice at Hazel's school, the sight of a 'Mickey Mouse' gas mask had precisely the opposite effect on one small boy to that which was intended. Instantly collapsing into hysterics, he had to be carried from the classroom struggling and screaming. The older children then took their masks from their boxes and put them on. As they breathed out through the snouts they found, to their delight, that they emitted a rude sound. Unison 'farting' was soon in progress, and so much mirth was caused that their visors were soon fogged up. As the days and weeks passed and the unfamiliar became

The following Public Air Raid Shelters are open continuously unless otherwise stated.

Map ref.   Map ref.

Address and number of persons   **Address and number of persons**

1	Late J. Farrar, Broad Street …250	12 Turners, 85 Pellon Lane (Bus. hrs. only) …100
2	Fields Chem.Works, Bull Close Lane …200	13 Pohlmanns, Princess St…115
3	Bull Green Lavatories …290	14 Sykes and Seed, 13 Square Road …300
4	Northern Academy Hairdressing, 17 Carlton Street…7	15 E.W. Collinson, St.John's Place …160
5	Clare Hall, Prescott Street …100	16 Webster's Warehouse, Pollard Street, off St. James' Road…260
6	Whitakers Brewery, Corporation Street (6 pm to 6 am) …150	17 Stannary Congregational Church…150
7	George Square Lavatories…60	18 Shay Tunnel …400
8	J. Haley, 40 Hopwood Lane …70	19 St.James' Vicarage, North Parade…130
9	North Bridge Arches …200	20 Tram Sheds …1,200
10	Stirrup, 22 North Parade …50	21 Lightowler and Co. Ltd, 1a Westfield Street…100
11	Under ARP Offices, Town Hall Street East …100	22 Kayll and Co., Weymouth Street …100
11	Lloyds Bank (ent. Northgate) …90	23 W. Rayner Ltd., Prince's Arcade, (Bus. hrs. only) …140
11	Watson's Gift Ex., off Northgate …65	24 Billiards Saloon, Arcade Royale, (Bus. hrs. only) …350
12	Beacon Radio, 75 Pellon Lane, (Bus. hrs. only) …32	25 W.D. Thwaite, 40 Northgate (Bus. hrs. only) …60

Where shelter could be found in central Halifax – October 1939.

the all too familiar, children soon saw how that mundane little box could be exploited. A late arrival at school could always be explained away with the words, "I forgot mi gas mask and I had to go back 'ome for it." A teacher could scarcely criticise obedience to government instructions! Much less fun was had when Hazel's father decided to run his own tests. Locking Hazel and her brother in the garden

shed, with only a smouldering sulphur pellet for company, he soon let them out because of the sheer panic that ensued in spite of the gas masks.

As it turned out, no gas attacks ever came and the masks became redundant. Germany had the technology and the means. Italy's dictator, Mussolini, had shown the devastating effects of poison gas used on helpless Abyssinian villagers in 1935. But the British weren't helpless; they could fight back. Perhaps it was Hitler's awareness of the very deadliness of this weapon that deterred him. The retaliation on German cities might well have had a catastrophic effect on civilian morale.

> *A mock gas attack in the centre of Todmorden caught both Vincent Holt and his mother without their gas masks. Even though they took refuge in a shop on Dale Street, Vincent was rash enough to take a deep sniff at the keyhole, inhaling enough tear gas to cause distress – a taste of the real thing.*

Nevertheless, gas was only one of the potential problems facing Civil Defence organisations in Britain. High explosive and incendiary bombs were two others. In February 1939, Halifax Town Council passed a £23,000 Air Raid Precaution project for the building of underground shelters in the centre of Halifax. By the end of October 1939, the Council was able to publish a location map showing where the public might seek refuge as a result of this now much extended scheme. On June 8th 1939, around 1,000 citizens of Queensbury and Shelf were treated to a novel event in a field at Roper Lane, Queensbury. As a police car broadcast an air raid siren on its loudspeaker, that mournful and eerie wail alternately rising and falling, six air raid wardens gave warning blasts on their whistles. The supposed incident was a high explosives bomb raid, resulting in injuries, disrupted utility services and a fire. The wardens demonstrated the use of stirrup pumps to deal with the fire and the control of a Thermite bomb with sand. Then, perhaps to the consternation of the crowd, a smoke bomb began to emit clouds of imitation chlorine gas and the wardens swiftly donned their gas masks. Interestingly enough, a declared aim of this demonstration was to try and make the public take air raid wardens seriously, for there had been a tendency to ridicule them. The public had to be convinced that there was another role for sand other than something to bury one's head in!

Apathy was not an accusation that could have been levelled at the 1,500 volunteers who, in 1939, had registered under Halifax's Air Raid Precaution (ARP) Officer, Mr L. Massey, and were being trained up for a range of duties on a part-time basis. From one end of Calderdale to the other a similar picture was emerging. What was probably not known to the general public was the degree to which plans had been laid down to cope with a possible crisis situation arising from a bombing raid. The Halifax ARP Emergency Committee, under Dr Hodge, had designated bases from which local services could be continued in the event of a breakdown of central control. These were at Belle Vue (then the Central Library), Princess Mary High School, Heath Grammar School and Bankfield Museum. News would be disseminated by loudspeaker vans which would range as far as Pye Nest, Wainstalls, Ovenden, Northowram and Southowram. Sixty-nine volunteers, comprising scouts and schoolchildren, would operate a bulletin posting service, as well as a 'telegram' service to keep people informed about missing relatives.

Civil Defence must be preceded by military defence. Information as to anti-aircraft installations was censored at the time, and difficult to obtain even after the war. However, the following were just some of the defences set up around our locality. There was said to have been a single searchlight and Lewis Gun emplacement at Savile Park in the earlier part of the war. There may also have been a searchlight battery at Roils Head playing fields and an anti-aircraft site at Highroad Well Moor. In the more outlying parts of the district, searchlights were noted in the football field at Hove Edge; at Blackshaw Head; on Centre Vale Park and on Todmorden Edge; and at Lane Bottom, Walsden, this one being accompanied by an anti-aircraft gun. Observation posts manned by the Royal Observer Corps were dotted at strategic points around the area. A more formidable presence was to be created later in the war when the 'Z' (Rocket) Battery was installed at Southowram.

HOW TO SMOTHER
A FIRE-BOMB

with half-filled sandbag and using dustbin lid as shield

(1) SHAKE SAND TO CENTRE of Bag.   (2) GRIP BOTH ENDS in one hand.

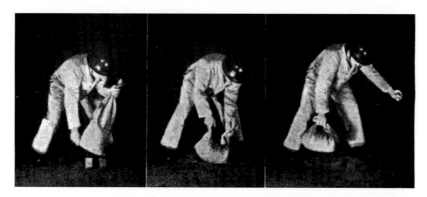

(3) USE DUSTBIN LID AS SHIELD.   (4) With SWING and STRIDE dump squarely on the bomb.

Grip BOTH ends of HALF–filled sandbag in one hand.	C R O U C H behind Dustbin Lid holding it WELL FORWARD.	Swing back then forward with a stride. Shield head and body to the last moment when bag takes place of lid as shield.	Dump bag squarely on the bomb and it will spread and completely cover it.

White lines show field of protection.   *Don't expose lower part of body by holding dustbin lid too high.*

Incendiaries could not be treated lightly

Courtesy of Calderdale MBC Libraries, Museums and Arts

There is little doubt, however, that in the early stages of the war at least, the rather flimsy defences around Halifax and Calderdale would have offered little more than, literally, 'a shot in the dark.' A determined enemy air attack would have got through. It was the first duty of ARP to try and protect the most vulnerable. Nobody could have been in a worse position than those rendered virtually immobile in hospital. On the first day of the war, September 3rd 1939, the Halifax Boys' Brigade, helped by other volunteers, were busy filling sandbags to protect the Royal Halifax Infirmary. It was felt too that those who would be tied to their duty posts during an air raid were entitled to some protection, and so civil defence posts and police stations were sandbagged wherever possible.

Anti-blast sandbagging at Brighouse police station.

Courtesy of Stephen Gee

Schoolchildren offered a particular headache for the authorities as large and vulnerable groups who could easily be caught up in a daytime raid. The extended school holidays of the summer of 1939 were intended to give the authorities the time to complete the building of air raid shelters at elementary schools. Stanley Topliss was a 10 year old attending Central Street School, Hebden Bridge, in 1939. Early

air raid drills involved trailing through the streets to the Hole-in-the-Wall pub and sitting cheek by jowl with the beer barrels in the cellars. Before the shelters had been built at Central Street, Stanley's family had moved

---

"young female teacher was reduced to hysterics"

---

house and he found himself attending Luddenden Foot Junior School. Here the shelters were dug into a field at the back, and on one occasion it was a question of who needed more protection, the teacher or the children? As the latter crowded inside, cheerful and chatty as usual, the door was banged. This raised the tension. Then, when Stanley put his ear to the ground and swore that he could hear bombs thudding down on Manchester, the young female teacher was reduced to hysterics. Luckily the children stayed calm!

The squat, rectangular brick buildings with concrete roofs that served as air raid shelters appeared in many schoolyards, but for some time at least Roomfield School, at Todmorden, was without them. As a child there, Eric Thomas was allocated a 'safe house' to run to in the event of an air raid. His was on Cambridge Street, presumably with a good cellar, and all Eric's fellow pupils were given 'safe house' addresses. They were also warned about the dangers of picking up 'butterfly' bombs, particularly unpleasant devices which posed a deadly threat to children, but which fortunately were only used once in a large scale in an attack on Hull.

Public air raid shelters came in all shapes and sizes. Factories could often provide their own basements as shelters, sometimes open to public use as well, such as at Victoria Mill in Hebden Bridge. Along Ovenden Way, orthodox surface shelters were to be found at intervals on the central reservation. Perhaps they were supplied by Fulcherite Ltd of Charlestown, Halifax, whose publicity stressed its expertise in reinforced concrete structures particularly suitable for ARP.

In the grounds of Brighouse Parish Hall a shelter was built up against the wall of the former National School. The railway arch at Scotty Bank, Brighouse, was another place of refuge.

Wherever possible, however, to get underground was the preferred option, such as in the Shay Tunnel beneath Skircoat Road, or under the Tram Sheds on Huddersfield Road, shown as numbers 18 and 20 on the town council's plan. Todmorden residents could disappear beneath their bus station. One ingenious adaptation was to use the base of a demolished mill chimney as a shelter, this being at Ivy House, Rastrick Common. As a teenager in Elland, Bertha Pottinger and her family were directed to use a quarry on Green Lane on one occasion when the sirens sounded.

Evidence that still remains – shelters for workers behind the former Furtex factory, Luddenden Foot.

Courtesy of the Longstaff Collection

The final problem in terms of air raid precaution, and perhaps the knottiest of all, was the protection of individual houses. The Halifax Town Council launched a programme of strengthening cellars with brick pillars and steel girders. Where no cellar existed, some families simply chose to sit under the stairs during an alert, or make a 'fun' cave out of the settee and armchairs. On the other hand, there were the famous Anderson Shelters. Sir John Anderson had been put in charge of ARP in November 1938 and he quickly approved of this relatively cheap, mass-produced home shelter for those without strong cellars, but with gardens. Anderson Shelters came in corrugated steel sections with sleeping bunks. They were free to manual workers in danger areas and to anyone earning less than £250 per annum, a skilled worker's wage at this time. For anyone else the cost varied between £6 14s and £10 18s, depending on size, although a 'six bunker' was the standard model.

By late 1939, 1,800 Anderson Shelters had arrived in Halifax. Geoff Whiteley's family lived on the Bracewell Estate (now gone) at Wheatley, and in common with most of their neighbours, the Whiteleys received a free Anderson Shelter. It arrived in sections, which had to be bolted together, and the trick lay in digging a hole deep enough in the garden to accommodate the bunks, leaving only the semi-circular steel roof above the ground. This was then usually covered with sandbags and earth. The final touch in wartime 'chic' décor was the flowerpot heater – a candle inside a flowerpot with an inverted one on top. Geoff's family was eight strong, and so it was a sizeable shelter, but they spent an enjoyable afternoon doing the job. After all that effort, however, the Whiteley family never spent a single night in their Anderson

Getting deep down in an Anderson Shelter.

Courtesy of Calderdale MBC Libraries, Museums and Arts

Shelter. They felt safe enough in bed although, ironically, the biggest bomb ever dropped locally during the war landed quite close to them. This one ton (1,000 kg) monster descended on the night of January 9th 1941, struck a greenhouse in a Wheatley garden and, luckily, failed to explode.

The ultimate solution for those who were determined to stay in their homes during air raids or alerts, but had no cellar, was the Morrison Shelter. Herbert Morrison was to succeed Sir John Anderson in 1941 as Home Secretary. The shelter which carried his name consisted of a large steel table at about normal table height. Underneath was a steel mattress, and all around was wire mesh. It could be used as a normal table during the day, but at night this structure, which resembled a rather glorified rabbit hutch, could accommodate two adults and two small children lying down. There were even two tier models for larger families.

Morrison Shelters came on the market from March 1941 – free to anyone earning less than £350 per annum; otherwise retailing at around £7.

The attractions of Morrisons as compared to Andersons were obvious. They were dual purpose, easy to erect and offered inside warmth and dryness. They were felt to be safer too. Outside surface shelters were not built to withstand direct hits. They were for protection against the flying debris of bomb blasts. The Anderson was no exception, for it was not far off being a surface shelter. However, it was far enough underground to make entombment a possibility in the event of explosions. The popularity of the Morrison was demonstrated by the fact that over 1,100,000 were in use by the end of the war.

Thus, by the early weeks of the Second World War, the ARP authorities of Halifax and Calderdale must have felt that they were reasonably well prepared for an air attack. The Halifax ARP Controller was the Town Clerk, Mr William Usher, and in Halifax alone he had seen the civil defence budget rise from around £14,000 per annum to £90,000 per annum. Joan Sutcliffe, from Pellon, was one of those who volunteered for ARP work during those anxious days. Working in the office at Asquith's by day, she attended a series of gas attack lectures at the ARP Training Centre in Hall Street, and

Volunteer 'victims' made local air raid wardens' drill more realistic.
Courtesy of Calderdale MBC Libraries, Museums and Art

soon found herself working two nights a week at the underground headquarters of Halifax ARP. This was situated at what was then known as the Tram Sheds at Huddersfield Road, and Joan's role on the central switchboard was to send out messages to dispatch riders on motor-bikes.

When the air raid sirens sounded in Halifax shortly after Neville Chamberlain's broadcast on September 3rd 1939, as part of a nation-wide testing of sirens, it was felt by many that the ARP volunteers would be called into action immediately. As night fell, tension rose. Many young people were only too willing to lend a hand and as a boy scout messenger and apprentice engineer, Ken Hirst spent an uneasy night in the underground shelter at the Tram Sheds. As the night passed on without incident, Ken eventually found some rest in the warmth of a single decker bus. It was the first of many nights to be spent like this for ARP personnel;

the 'phoney war' had begun. Joan Sutcliffe found that the majority of messages she was transmitting to her motor cyclists concerned blackout transgressions.

> *On October 22nd 1939, the borough held its largest ARP exercise yet, involving a total of 1,800 volunteers, including members of the Auxiliary Fire and Ambulance Services. The usual threats were simulated – high explosive bombs, incendiaries, mustard gas – and 150 boy scouts enthusiastically participated as 'casualties.' These littered the streets moaning realistically, with little cards attached to them bearing such gruesome descriptions as, 'left arm torn off,' 'guts hanging out.'*

In spite of the government's wish that the nation should not drop its guard, a tendency to cynicism began to creep in amongst the public. The only real ARP activity seemed to be a

Confidential

AIR RAID PRECAUTIONS
TRAINING PAMPHLET No. 3

ADVISING THE PUBLIC IN THE EVENT OF INVASION

(NOTES FOR THE GUIDANCE OF AIR RAID WARDENS)

Issued by the Ministry of Home Security

But the public didn't seem to be listening during the 'phoney war.'
Courtesy of Calderdale MBC Libraries, Museums and Arts

stringent enforcement of the blackout regulations, and as the number of fines rose, so did public resentment. ARP wardens were issued with a training pamphlet, 'Advising the Public in the Event of an Invasion,' but the public seemed to be asking no questions about a prospective invasion. The only question being asked was whether all this blackouting and taping up of windows was necessary at all. There were some full-time wardens, paid at £3 per week, and the 'Daily Express' began a campaign against the "darts and playing cards army." In some instances, air raid wardens did not help themselves by being unnecessarily officious, or even inefficient. Margaret Hitchen, saw this negative side when, around 1940, a little localised exercise took place in the Bell Hall area of Halifax. Four streets were evacuated due to the supposed dropping of an incendiary bomb. "Several middle-aged to elderly men in tin hats rushed around self-importantly and we all waited for the explosion." However, no matter what they did, the men in tin hats could not induce the bomb to explode. Meanwhile the onlookers were gradually reduced to helpless laughter.

> *The sense of unreality induced by the 'phoney war' pervaded government circles too. The lack of German air raids prompted some to think that perhaps Britain should take the initiative, and Kingsley Wood, Secretary for Air, proposed setting fire to the Black Forest with incendiaries. Several MP's were aghast at the idea. "Are you not aware it is private property?" said one.*

The 'phoney war' lasted almost a year, giving Britain precious time both to complete her air defences and build more fighter aircraft. The lull ended with German attacks on convoys in the Channel in July 1940, and the epic 'Battle of Britain,' fought in the skies above South East England during August and September. It was, however, the 'blitz' which turned air raid wardens 'from zeros to heroes' overnight. From September 7th to November 2nd 1940, London was bombed every night.

The heavy bombing spread to provincial cities, and the ARP system, linked with the Auxiliary Fire and Ambulance Services, really began to show its worth. And yet as far as Halifax and Calderdale were concerned, the enemy remained an invisible one. He was there in the sky somewhere, thousands of feet up, but he was discerned by sound rather than sight – the dull, heavy throb of laden bombers at night. Their flight path to Manchester passed directly above the Upper Calder Valley and it was from vantage points here that people could see, way beyond Stoodley Pike, the aftermath of their passing – the red glow of a burning city.

Invisible he might be, but the enemy was getting closer. The first local bombs of the war fell as the 'phoney war' drew to a close. At around 1 am on June 28th 1940, eight bombs fell harmlessly on moorland near Gorple Reservoir. Almost two months later, on 24th August, seven bombs fell near Walterclough, Southowram, but damage was limited to the severing of an overhead power cable and the breaking of a few windows.

> *According to one local resident, the Walterclough bombs came as a result of the searchlight on the football pitch at Hove Edge picking up a German fighter-bomber, which then dived down the beam and let loose its bombs. As the next day was Sunday, much of the local population descended on the area around 'Sunny Bunce's' looking for souvenir shrapnel.*

A few days later, on August 29th 1940, three bombs fell in a field between Ox Heys Farm, Shelf, and Norwood Green, resulting in some broken windows. Around midnight on 6th September, several flares and incendiaries fell on Bell House Moor, on the Erringden side of Mytholmroyd. Not only did they provide a spectacular 'fireworks' display, but the moorland was also set alight in several places.

In a sense, so far so good; nobody even injured and no real damage done. The 'blitz' had not yet begun, and the German bombing seemed random, small-scale and ineffectual.

Surely Bell House and Gorple Moors were not prime targets in the Luftwaffe's grand scheme of things. Nevertheless random bombs by their very nature are unpredictable. Whilst the 'blitz' raged elsewhere, it was over two months before another bomb was to fall locally, but this time the invisible enemy delivered a single blow with devastating force at the very heart of Halifax.

At around 9 pm on Friday November 22nd 1940, the audience at the Palace, Halifax, heard a faint but distinct thud. A few quizzical looks were exchanged, but as there was no pause in the show and no member of the management came on stage to announce an air raid alert, people settled back in their seats to enjoy the rest of the show. Mary Crossley was among them and at the end of the performance she set off in the total darkness of the blackout towards her home at Oak Terrace, off Hanson Lane. Her first task, however, would be to pick up her baby, who was being taken care of by Mary's mother at her home in Hanson Lane. Alarm bells began to ring in Mary's head as she found the bottom of Hanson Lane cordoned off. ARP workers directed her up Pellon Lane and along Queen's Road in order to enter Hanson Lane higher up. Here she began to encounter a little wreckage, but she was relieved to find both her mother and her baby safe and asleep at Hanson Lane. Mary retired to bed little wiser than before.

It was not until the following morning, when Mary went down Hanson Lane to shop at the

"She encountered a scene of ruin and devastation"

Economic Stores, that she was able to appreciate the full impact of the previous night's events. She encountered a scene of ruin and devastation. The Hanson Lane bomb is the single most memorable event of the wartime years locally in that it has entered the common 'folk memory' of a generation. Certain inescapable facts emerge, but around them swirl a mix of personal recollection, hearsay

and rumour which combine to provide a fascinating story. In the realm of the strictly factual, a single 220 lbs (100 kg) bomb fell on the night of Friday November 22nd 1940. It hit the pavement outside 77 Hanson Lane, almost opposite the end of Crossley Terrace. The bomb was a relatively small one, but in the confined space of this densely packed area, it did colossal damage. The blast damaged 537 houses, so badly in the case of 37 that they were rendered uninhabitable. Some of these simply had to be demolished. In the light of the destruction, casualties were relatively light – 11 killed and 10 needing hospital treatment - but a high rate considering that only one bomb exploded.

So tight was the censorship of the time, that even the 'Halifax Courier and Guardian' was only able to refer to this incident as 'Raid on Northern Town.' The report was graphic, however, in its description of how the blast had ripped out the frontage of a block of four houses and shops. A similar block opposite, which included the West Hill Hotel, a public house, was also heavily damaged. These eight premises had to be pulled down a few days later. The bomb dropped directly in front of a shop owned by the Burrows family, which had been open for business, but fortunately the other three premises in the block of four had no occupants at the time.

The shock waves from the explosion radiated outwards rapidly and a grocer's shop at the junction of Hanson Lane and Crossley Terrace, belonging to Mr and Mrs John Peat, took the full brunt. It was almost completely wrecked and was another of the properties which later had to be demolished. The roofs of

" the street was littered with glass, window frames, doors, slates and stones.

20 houses on Crossley Terrace were lifted, and flying slates joined the glass that was hurtling through the air in spite of many windows having been criss-crossed with tape or covered with netting. From Raglan Street to Brinton

The appalling effects of the high explosive on Hanson Lane.

Courtesy of Calderdale MBC Libraries, Museums and Arts

Terrace, a distance of about 200 yards, the street was littered with glass, window frames, doors, slates and stones. Windows were broken as far away as Pellon Lane, Highroad Well and even Ovenden.

So much for the plain facts, but it is not too difficult to imagine both the mental and physical shock that were visited on the residents of the area that night. No bomb had ever fallen on Halifax; no bomb had fallen in the vicinity for over two months. ARP had been alerted to the presence of an enemy aircraft overhead, but to those in the Hanson Lane area, the first intimation of any real danger was the whistle of the descending bomb. It is not difficult either to imagine the fear and confusion which followed the attack. With death and destruction everywhere, people had to grope about in the darkness, often choked by

billowing clouds of soot from chimneys. No lights had to be shown outside for fear of inviting another aerial attack. Even domestic fires had to be covered or doused. How difficult must it have been to maintain a blackout with one's windows and doors blown off? The situation was not helped by sightseers flooding into the area until the streets were cordoned off.

However, the moment had come for the rescue services – the police, air raid wardens and the Auxiliary Fire and Ambulance Services. All their training was put into effect. This was a world away from treating boy scout 'casualties' on a civil defence exercise, but by all accounts the rescue services arrived promptly and, even in total darkness, worked efficiently. A fire at the immediate scene of the explosion was quickly extinguished, and the local air raid warden's post served as a dressing

The Halifax Auxiliary Ambulance Service came into its own during the Hanson Lane incident.

Courtesy of Calderdale MBC Libraries, Museums and Arts

station for minor injuries. The butt of jokes only twelve months earlier, the wardens now found themselves being asked for advice and assistance from all sides.

Of those killed, three of the victims were found in the rubble of the Burrows' shop, outside which the bomb had detonated. Three men in the parlour of the West Hill, immediately adjacent to Hanson Lane, were killed, one of them being decapitated. The licensee, Mr Garforth, was serving in the bar when he saw the front of the building apparently disintegrating and rushing towards him. Miraculously he escaped with cuts, although he required much stitching up. A man waiting for the Norton Tower bus on Raglan Street was killed.

> *The best known story to emerge from the Hanson Lane episode concerns a 16 year old butcher's boy, 'Sapho' Pearson. Having left work to catch his bus home, he realised that he had forgotten his wages and returned to the shop. The delay caused him to miss his bus and he was killed waiting for the next one. The butcher's shop on Hanson Lane was owned by Geoffrey and Rachel Thompson, father of Donald Thompson, who later became a local MP.*

The Hanson Lane bomb left such a vivid imprint on the minds of the people of Halifax that stories abound about the incident, little cameos illustrating the ironies of life, the freakishness of chance and how apparently trivial decisions can sometimes have profound consequences. How ironic, for example, that a Mr William Barrett had come from the Midlands partly to escape the bombing and had settled near to Hanson Lane. However, he lived to tell the tale. How freakish that a blast strong enough to wreck the front portion of the West Hill did not spill a drop of the glasses of beer which stood in the back room; did not even crack a window on the bus approaching nearby Raglan Street, but knocked a man off his ladder who was whitewashing a cellar a quarter of a mile away.

It was also a mere matter of chance which, in all probability, saved the life of a Halifax fireman, Tom Peploe, and that of his driver George Kay. A 'yellow' alert, signifying a German aircraft in the vicinity, meant that the fire-fighters at Beech Hill fire station, Pellon Lane, had to travel to their stand-by base at Whitley's Mills, Hanson Lane. As the line of vehicles moved out of Beech Hill, the front one stalled. A few minutes were lost, meaning that the convoy had only got half-way along Raglan Street when the bomb fell. Those 'precious minutes' lost at Beech Hill may well have meant precious lives saved.

One rumour concerning the Hanson Lane bomb still persists to this day and it arose because of the apparent oddness of a German aircraft dropping only a single bomb rather than a 'stick' of several. From this, a theory has grown that the bomb was 'one of ours,' what we would call today 'friendly fire.' It is not so odd to think of a German aircraft returning from a raid on Manchester, slightly lost

A seemingly trivial decision almost certainly saved Philip Hanson's mother, Ada, from death or serious injury. Friday night was her usual night for travelling down from Pellon to visit a lady friend who lived on the corner of Hanson Lane and Crossley Terrace. Ada always came home on the 9 pm bus. However, for some reason she decided to give the visit a miss on this occasion.

perhaps, carrying a bomb which for some reason had not been released with the rest over the target. Certainly the local ARP units had been made aware of enemy activity in the sky via the 'yellow' alert signal. Perhaps a chink of light was spotted below, or maybe it was just random chance that sent the bomb whistling down on Hanson Lane. Whatever the truth, for the people of Halifax the main question now was whether this bomb would be the first of many. Had the Halifax 'blitz' begun?

THE STORM DOES NOT BREAK

"We have not forgotten toffee town." 'Lord Haw-Haw.'

The days and nights which followed November 22nd 1940 were anxious ones for the people of Halifax and Calderdale, particularly the nights. As dusk fell, apprehensive looks were cast at the sky. Ears were more finely attuned to that heavy drone of a Junkers, a Heinkel or a Dornier. Out on the streets, there was a keener awareness as to the location of the nearest air raid shelter. After all, 'Lord Haw-Haw,' the notorious pro-German radio propagandist, was heard to say, "We have not forgotten toffee town," widely interpreted as meaning Halifax. Was the storm about to

---

"night after night, the bombers pounded British towns and cities."

---

break? These were difficult and depressing days generally. Britain and her Empire stood totally alone against Hitler and Mussolini, whilst in the Far East the rising menace of Japan cast an increasingly long shadow. In spite of the inspiring and constantly optimistic words of Churchill, victory seemed a remote prospect. For the moment, the best that could be hoped for was to keep Germany at bay, and in the meantime, night after night, the bombers pounded British towns and cities. For Halifax, however, the storm never really broke. Air raids did not end with the Hanson Lane bomb, but what followed was not a sustained onslaught, more a series of intermittent inconveniences, with no human casualties.

The most serious threat was posed early in 1941. Phyllis Stead, who was running a butcher's shop at Pye Nest all on her own after her husband's 'call-up' into the forces, was walking along Edwards Road at around 8 pm on January 9th 1941. She was going for a bus and in the company of a "spiritualist lady" of her acquaintance. The latter claimed to have some sort of psychic insight, and she warned Phyllis to look out for fires that night. Not long afterwards a shower of incendiary bombs fell across King Cross and West End. Whilst being impressed at the accuracy of the prediction, Phyllis was a little bemused by the fact that one of the incendiaries had gone through the roof of the spiritualist lady's house on Edwards Road, thus proving that to be forewarned was not necessarily to be forearmed.

WHERE THE BOMBS DROPPED

16th December 1940
Several bombs fell on moorland at Walsden. One casualty – a duck.

9th January 1941 8.10 pm
Hundreds of incendiaries showered King Cross and West End. One 1,000 kg bomb was discharged, but did not explode after landing in a Wheatley allotment.

14th March 1941 (night)
Bombs fell at Stump Cross, Hawes Lane and Salterlee. About 26 people were temporarily evacuated and Salterlee Lodge had to be demolished. A few incendiaries also fell at Northowram and Shelf.

14th March 1941 (night)
"Molotov Baskets" and incendiary bombs, mostly dud, fell on Hameldon Hill near Gorple.

12th August 1942 1.40 am – 2.35 am
14 flares lit up a hillside at Sowerby between Beechwood and Steep Lane.

24th December 1944 5.30 am
A flying bomb landed in a field at Little Toothill Farm, Hubberton, Sowerby. The farmhouse was extensively damaged, and windows broken one mile away.

The hundreds of incendiaries that fell could have been a prelude to a more serious attack. Joan Sutcliffe not only did voluntary night duty on the switchboard at ARP headquarters at the Tram Sheds, but she was also on the fire-watching rota at her old school, Princess Mary.

What do I do...

when I hear short blasts on whistles?

I remember that this is no longer merely a signal for an air-raid "alert." *It means that fire-bombs are falling.*

So whenever I hear whistles, night or day, I keep a sharp look-out for fire-bombs.

If I see them, I remember it is my duty to help in tackling them—watchers or no watchers. So I get to know where the nearest fire-fighting appliances are.

And I remember — "Soon tackled, soon out."

Cut this out—and keep it !

Issued by The Ministry of Information

Space presented to the Nation by the Brewers' Society

This new fire-bomb warning system came just in the nick of time for King Cross and West End.

She was on duty here on the night of January 9th 1941, and in her view the raid was probably targeting Halifax's engineering works. The bombs that came down on West End fell across the top end of Parkinson Lane, Gibraltar Road and on towards Wellesley Park Barracks. Apart from causing fires and confusion, the aim of incendiary bombs was to illuminate the target for more bombers to follow on and drop their high explosives.

Fortunately, at this very time the government had begun to give much higher priority to fire-watching, and all males aged between 16 and 60, who were not engaged in Civil Defence or Home Guard duties, were compelled to undertake 48 hours fire-watching per month, during night hours. The pay for this was 1s 6d (7.5p) per night. That very week, advice had been given to groups of Civil Defence volunteers from every street in Halifax as to how to deal with fire bombs. The fire-watchers around King Cross and West End did their bit on the night of 9th January. The new signal of short blasts on whistles by air raid wardens was heeded and within fifteen minutes, with the use of sandbags and stirrup pumps, the fires were quelled - not a moment too soon. Shortly afterwards another bomber passed overhead, making it more than likely that this was a planned attack rather than a random or accidental dropping of incendiaries.

Not only this, the same night of January 9th was the one during which a one ton (1,000 kg) bomb came crashing down through a greenhouse in a Wheatley garden. This may have come from the aircraft which was unable to find its targets around the King Cross and West End areas, or from another plane, but it does show that Halifax was the subject of some special enemy attention that night. The owner of the greenhouse was a Mr Albert Holdsworth, who was in Halifax town centre when the sirens went, and decided to return to what he considered to be a safer place, his home in Wheatley. As he approached his house, however, he heard the whistle of a falling bomb, followed by the crash and thud of its landing nearby. Assuming that the noise had been that of an explosion, Albert went to bed

Is your
STIRRUP PUMP
ready for
immediate action?

Will it pull out straight
. . . . without a kink?
Or will it be in a muddle?
. . . . or a spiral?

Learn to Coil it Correctly

1. Pull the hose out straight, without kinks (This is essential).
2. Place left foot on stirrup, so that you **can step forward** with **right foot.** Steady pump with left hand.
3. Using right hand to coil hose into left hand, make one straightforward coil.
4. Reach well forward with right hand <u>under</u> the long end of the hose and with <u>palm downwards.</u> With a twist of the <u>wrist</u> grip the hose; then, turning the knuckles uppermost (thumb pointing away from body) transfer the <u>inward</u> coil, thus formed, to the left hand.
5. Continue ALTERNATELY straightforward and inward coils.
6. Secure hose in position with tape or strap that can be undone in a moment.

Don't trip over your stirrup pump.

Courtesy of Calderdale MBC Libraries, Museums and Arts

that Thursday night counting his lucky stars for a near miss. The weekend was to show how near the miss had been, for on entering his garden the following Saturday, Albert found that only half his greenhouse was standing. The rest was inside a crater.

Albert duly reported his findings to the police, and on the Sunday decided to make the best of a bad job. He decided that the hole would be the ideal receptacle for garden

"unaware that he was leaping about above a one ton unexploded bomb,"

rubbish. Topping it off with soil, he did something then that might have given Albert's story an abrupt ending. He vigorously began to stamp the soil down to get a firm surface, unaware that he was leaping about above a one ton unexploded bomb, almost five times as large as the one that had devastated the Hanson Lane area. When the bomb disposal experts arrived on the Monday, they quickly realised what was likely to be resting under all the rubbish, and their jaws progressively dropped as Albert told his hair-raising tale. Everyone had to sit down and take a few deep breaths before the bomb disposal team, with meticulous care, set to work.

The bombs which fell later, on the night of March 14th 1941, did no real damage. Nevertheless, routines for dealing with aerial attack had to be made as near perfect as possible, and because of the large-scale use of incendiary bombs, this was as true for the Auxiliary Fire Service as for the air raid wardens. There was no doubt about the seriousness of the training, as one young man from Southowram found when he chose the Fire Service as his form of 'National Service.' His headquarters was a large empty warehouse in the middle of Brighouse which had been fitted out as an auxiliary fire station to supplement the regular full-time fire brigade. Training took place on three nights per week, plus Sundays. The canal towpath at Brighouse was an ideal place for learning how to use all the fire appliances. Much time was spent in practising connecting up hoses and pumping water across town and up steep hillsides. The lake at Crow Nest Mansion, Lightcliffe, was also used by the Auxiliary Fire Service for training purposes.

In common with the Home Guard, the AFS often found itself engaged in night movements at weekends in order to see how

> *Carrying heavy men down ladders from the roofs of high buildings; crawling through a narrow shed with fires burning at the sides; all was part of the training routine for the would-be fireman.*

efficiently it functioned in blackout conditions. Local ARP authorities were always anxious to simulate the 'real thing' in large-scale combined operations involving the fire, ambulance and police services, along with air raid wardens, the Home Guard, the Women's Voluntary Service and volunteer 'casualties.' Halifax held a big Civil Defence exercise in October 1941 and a 'blitz' weekend in July 1942. Later that year, Brighouse and Elland combined in an 'invasion test,' whilst Queensbury and Shelf held its own 'blitz' exercise.

The AFS was often very simply equipped – usually a hose and pump on the back of a converted vehicle or trailer. This was partly for reasons of economy, and partly for ease of movement through streets that might be partly blocked by rubble. However, they would carry no water, unlike regular fire engines, and so large static water tanks were set up at numerous locations. Another advantage of small-scale was that these fire pumps could be stored in

This Auxiliary Fire Service vehicle attended the area's only V1 incident.
Courtesy of Calderdale MBC Libraries, Museums and Arts

garages or outbuildings virtually anywhere. To be a member of the AFS, however, meant to be always 'on call.' Donald Shaw had joined the family soft drinks firm in Halifax on leaving school. After serving in the Home Guard for a spell, he joined the AFS and put one of the firm's wagons at the disposal of the service. It was to be used to pull a trailer with fire-fighting equipment on board, and Donald would do the driving. Every time the sirens sounded, it was his job to walk from his home in Copley to where the vehicles were stored, behind the Falcon Inn at Salterhebble. There he had to remain until the 'all-clear' sounded. On one particular night, he had to do this on three occasions. After the third time, almost sleepwalking home, he vowed that enough was enough. Siren or no siren he was not getting up again! Luckily, (as far as he knew) the sirens stayed quiet for what was left of the night.

A Fire Service dispatch rider making a splash at Elphin Brook, Mytholmroyd.

On the other hand Milton Sunderland, of Mytholmroyd, found that he was able to combine his two major hobbies – motor-cycles and guns – through his membership of the National Fire Service. Milton was no ordinary motor-cyclist. In pre-war days he had built up a reputation at the Isle of Man TT Races. He had also ridden the 'Wall of Death' at Belle Vue, Manchester, and performed as a stunt rider at galas. When the opportunity came, during the war, to become section leader of a group of Fire Service dispatch riders to cover the Calder Valley area, it was too good to miss. If the telephone lines became in any way disrupted, it was the job of his team to carry essential messages and information. If the main road through the Calder Valley was blocked also, then the dispatch riders would be able to use minor roads and tracks. To Milton, exercises and practice runs with his team were much more of a pleasure than a duty. In fact, he was in his element. Was that enough for him? Not quite.

One specialised role that had been assigned to Milton rested on his pre-war exploits as a stunt rider. It was his job to investigate any reports of planes crashing on the local moors, and this would inevitably involve some 'rough riding' across country. Milton was happy to do this, but pointed out to his chiefs that if the plane happened to be a German one, then any survivors would be armed, which would put him at a distinct disadvantage. He persuaded them that as a small arms expert and enthusiast,

Milton Sunderland – without his Mauser on this occasion.

he could be trusted to carry a gun. Reluctantly they agreed, and from that point the flamboyant Milton cut a dashing figure as he roared around the countryside with a Mauser automatic pistol strapped to his waist in a holster, somewhat like a motorised sheriff. He never used the gun in anger, but claimed to be the only armed fireman in the country.

The period between March 1941 and August 1942 saw a long lull in terms of local air raids. The 'blitz' as a sustained assault had faded away nationally, along with the threat of invasion. However, it was wise not to be complacent. In the early hours of August 12th 1942, the Upper Calder Valley was illuminated by a strange and garish light as 14 candle flares descended between Beechwood and Steep Lane at Sowerby. The purpose of this was unclear, but according to an ARP Reconnaissance Officer at Mytholmroyd, the flares were accompanied by two 'Flam C 500' parachute mines filled with incendiary bombs. If this was the case, little or no damage seems to have been done. The effectiveness of the flares was such, however, that from the light cast out the officer was able to make an entry in his notebook and read a newspaper at Mytholmroyd Post Office.

An even longer lull followed, from August 1942 to December 1944. Gas mask cases were being used as lunch boxes, and people tended not to move from their beds when the air raid sirens were sounded, as they still were from time to time. After 'D-Day' on June 6th 1944, and the opening of the Second Front in Occupied Europe, it seemed only a matter of time before Germany would be defeated. ARP personnel, however, needed to stay vigilant. Hitler had been threatening Britain with his 'secret weapons,' and although this was dismissed by many as the desperate but idle talk of a doomed dictator, intelligence reports indicated that Germany might well be on the point of using her 'vengeance weapons.' This was indeed the case, and on June 13th 1944, the first V1 flying bomb fell on London. These vicious, small-scale pilotless aircraft, with their stubby wings, were packed with high explosive and they could cause immense damage.

The peculiar drone of V1s caused them to be named 'buzz bombs' or, more oddly, 'doodlebugs.' They had the unnerving habit of coming any time, day or night, and a terrible silence always hung in the air between the cutting out of a V1's engine and the sound of the explosion.

A total of 6,184 people were killed by these flying bombs, almost all in London. However, by August 1944, 80% of them were being destroyed by fighter aircraft or anti-aircraft guns. The people of Halifax and Calderdale may by then have been feeling relatively safe, but there was a little 'sting in the tail' for the district. Early on the morning of December 24th 1944, a group of specially adapted Heinkel bombers released around forty V1s off the Yorkshire Coast, with the probable target of Manchester. Roy Newbitt, living at Old Town above Hebden Bridge, had been awoken by a mouse rooting around in a cardboard box when he heard the distinctive 'chugging' of a flying bomb overhead. As a fire service messenger, his duty was to report what he had heard, and he emerged from his house at around 5.30 am on a foggy morning, just as another 'buzz bomb' went over.

In all, Roy must have heard six or seven of them passing across the Calder Valley as he attempted in vain to contact his fellow Old Town fire-fighters. He assumed that the Manchester region was their target, but as he discussed this with Mrs Hope, the local headmaster's wife, whom he found peering into the fog outside the school, they both heard yet another 'doodlebug,' this time passing over Mount Skip. Then, heart stoppingly, the engine cut out. Shortly afterwards came a huge flash followed by a tremendous bang. It was clear that the flying bomb had come down somewhere on the Sowerby hillside, but even in Old Town windows vibrated with the shock.

In fact, the bomb had skimmed the chimney pots of the Triangle Road district of Sowerby and landed in a field a short distance from Little Toothill Farm, Hubberton. The building had its roof and doors blown in, and the barn was

Little Toothill Farm, Hubberton, after a V1 flying bomb had landed nearby.

Courtesy of Calderdale MBC Libraries, Museums and Arts

All in all, then, Halifax and its surrounding district escaped the heavy bombing that was feared, if not seriously expected. As suggested earlier, perhaps the Luftwaffe had other priorities in terms of targets. Perhaps also, precise objectives were difficult to achieve when West Riding towns such as Halifax, Bradford and Huddersfield were clustered so closely together. Even when the Germans began to use radio beam navigation instead of the stars, British scientists invented techniques to mislead the bombers. There

partially demolished. The occupants, Mr and Mrs Jack Carter, were in bed at the time of impact, and received cuts from flying glass in a blast that was powerful enough to break windows up to a mile away, and render Little Toothill Farm temporarily uninhabitable. This V1 carried something a little more than high explosive. Propaganda leaflets, entitled 'V-Post,' were scattered over a wide area around the huge crater. They purported to be copies of letters written by British prisoners-of-war in Germany, and there were also magazines containing photographs of Allied leaders, accompanied by threats of the dire punishments they would face, "when Germany wins the war." This gives some idea of the dual purpose of the V1 campaign – to spread both terror and propaganda.

was talk too during the war of something mysterious having been built on the moors near Blackstone Edge, a dummy airfield being the best local guess, at any rate something which might explain why more bombs seemed to be hitting the moors than the streets. The rumours were a little wide of the mark, but there certainly was a top-secret establishment on the moors. However, it was nearly 50 years after the war had ended before the moorland mystery was satisfactorily solved, and the credit for unravelling it must go to Halifax Antiquarian, Mr Donald Haigh.

The location of the establishment was Cragg Vale rather than Blackstone Edge, and it was not a 'dummy airfield' but one of the Air Ministry's improbably named 'Starfish' sites – a decoy for an important civilian target. 'Starfish' sites aimed at diverting German night bombers from their real targets by simulating urban lighting, including that of factories and transport networks, so that they could best be described as 'decoy towns.' Fires could also be lit to imitate the large cigar pattern of a stick of incendiary bombs, thus further encouraging the main force to expend its high explosive bombs on the decoy.

The hiker following the Calderdale Way across the bleak tract of land between Mill

> *Each V1 was fitted with a wind driven device that cut off the fuel at a distance calculated for the 'doodlebug' to fall on its target. This suggests that the Hubberton bomb, together with others that morning, were faulty. Nevertheless, for towns such as Sowerby Bridge and Halifax it was a narrow escape from a much more devastating version of the Hanson Lane incident.*

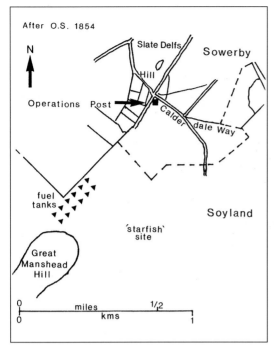

Cragg Vale's top secret 'Starfish' site.

Courtesy of Donald Haigh

Bank and Cragg Vale would see little to suggest that this rough pasture and moorland was a wartime hive of activity. One clue remains, however. On the moorland edge, at Slate Delfs Hill, is a small ruin which looks for all the world like an air raid shelter. But an air raid shelter on the moors? Nevertheless it is constructed of bricks, has a flat concrete roof, is sunk within earth banks, and in front of its only entrance is a blast protection wall. In fact, this structure was once the operations control post for the Cragg Vale 'Starfish' site. To have freely walked across this area when the site was operational would have been impossible. Entry was barred to all except the twenty or so authorised RAF personnel. Harsher still, any occupant of a farm within the designated area was simply evicted. This was the fate of Peter Sugden's family at Slate Delfs Farm. His father was halfway through a rental purchase scheme when the men from the Ministry arrived. The Sugdens left and were never able to return, the farm lying derelict for something like 50 years, until its relatively recent restoration.

By the end of 1942, there were 235 'Starfish' sites across Britain. Calderdale contained two, one at Cragg Vale and another at Clifton. Virtually nothing is known about the latter site other than that it was situated at the edge of Clifton Common, and was operational from April 1941 to March 1942. The site at Cragg Vale was operational from about the same time and abandoned in June 1943, by which time the Germans had lost air superiority. Local oral evidence suggests that the site was manned by about twenty airmen taking turns on duty, and it housed about a dozen square tanks filled with oil, roughly situated towards Great Manshead Hill, as shown on the sketch map. Shortly after the end of the European war, in May 1945, the 'Courier' took up the theme, describing these as flare pans, full of oil and old rubber tyres. The newspaper account also mentions 'skeleton' structures, created to look like real buildings. The operations control post at Slate Delfs Hill was the 'brain' of the site. This was where the electricity was generated both to ignite the flare pans and to trigger the decoy lighting.

Standing now on this bleak stretch of Pennine moorland at around 1,200 feet, it is difficult to envisage it as it once was. All that remains is the ruin of the operations control post. And yet, within that dereliction lay the means to illuminate the moorland towards

"decoy for Greetland station and railway marshalling yards."

Great Manshead with fires that could simulate a pattern of incendiary bombs, thus decoying night bombers from their target. But what might that target have been? The answer is perhaps a surprising one. The Cragg Vale 'Starfish' site was a decoy for Greetland station and railway marshalling yards. The distance of six miles between decoy and target may seem considerable, but not for an aircraft flying at around four miles a minute. The surprise lies in the fact that the long redundant Greetland station and marshalling yards were once important enough to merit such protection. The

The remains of the operations control post clearly show the blast protection wall.

Photograph by Alexander Thomas

On the night of January 21st 1943, a Halifax bomber was returning from mine-laying operations off the

"dangerously high ground near Hebden Bridge"

Friesian Islands when it overshot its base at Snaith, near Selby. Unbeknown to the crew, the plane was in the vicinity of dangerously high ground near Hebden Bridge, and at 10.25 pm the Halifax struck a dry-stone wall on Hoar Side Moor, between Blackshaw Head and Gorple Upper Reservoir. It skidded across the flat moor and came to rest in a shallow stream before bursting into flames. Two of the crew of seven either died on impact or were engulfed in the fire that totally destroyed the plane. There were almost certainly mines still on board the plane, which would have ensured its total destruction.

The second incident involved an American B-24 Liberator based at North Pickenham, Norfolk. The story of how it arrived on our local moors is one that illustrates the strange and tragic ironies that war can throw up. The plane was due for maintenance at its base depot at Burtonwood and its American pilot, First Lieutenant Charles Goeking, would have

decoy lighting would probably have been on the lines of simulated locomotive firebox glows and a pattern of hooded lamps. Any 'skeleton' structures present must have been imitations of railway sheds or the like. As it turned out, the Cragg Vale 'Starfish' site was never attacked by enemy bombers and so the flare pans may never have been ignited in earnest, but nor did any bombs fall on the Greetland marshalling yards.

Incendiary bombs and flares did land on our local moorland, particularly between 1940 and 1941, but in such a random way as to suggest that high moors and deep valleys had a confusing effect on German bombers. This was often compounded by low clouds and moorland mist. It is not surprising that enemy navigators encountered problems, for the treacherous combination of local topography and capricious weather even brought two Allied aircraft to grief during the war. Once again, wartime censorship left people to speculate as to the exact details of these crashes, but investigations in recent years have brought the truth to light.

The Liberator that was to break itself on Black Hameldon Hill.

Courtesy of Nick Wotherspoon at 'LAIT'

regarded the trip there from North Pickenham as a 'milk run,' especially as he had just arrived back from leave too late to take part in the apparently much more dangerous mission of bombing marshalling yards in Germany.

The Liberator set off on the afternoon of February 19th 1945 with a crew of five, plus six passengers who were 'hitching' a ride to Burtonwood. As the plane crossed the Pennines, the weather took a hand, with low cloud, rain and fog shrouding the landscape. Descending through a break in the cloud at 4.25 pm, the pilot mistook the towns of Accrington and Burnley for the Liverpool conurbation. Climbing again, he made a 90 degree turn to the right towards what he believed was the direction of Burtonwood, and flew at full power towards Black Hameldon Hill on the borderland between Calderdale and Burnley. Aware at the last moment of the dark shadow of the hill in front of him, the pilot tried to climb, and so it was the tail which made first impact, instantly breaking the plane in two. Five American airmen were killed, three died of injuries, and three survived, although with major injuries. The pilot, Charles Goeking, was one of the survivors, having miraculously escaped death even though he had been hurled through the armoured windscreen. He was hospitalised for two years.

Censorship there might have been, but news of this nature soon gets around. Schoolboys from both sides of the county border were soon swarming over the crashed Liberator. One can assume that they were not indifferent to the human cost, but as is the way with youngsters, this was soon pushed to the backs of their minds in the frenzied hunt for souvenirs. Vincent Holt and his friends made the trip over the moors from Todmorden and, incredibly enough, met a schoolboy acquaintance carting away a dismounted machine gun and a belt of ammunition. The police caught up with him the same day and, armed with information

Engines from the stricken Liberator.
Courtesy of Nick Wotherspoon at 'LAIT'

received, were soon visiting a number of addresses to retrieve some of the more important or dangerous items looted from the plane. Vincent's find was harmless enough – a small survival kit comprising a compass and matches that would light even when wet – a curio which he kept for many years. He was told that the kit allowed crash survivors to set fire to the plane and then find their way to safety.

Collectors of militaria may well have felt deprived in comparison with those who lived in the areas where the air battles raged in the early stages of the war. However, even before the war had ended, interesting items began to arrive in local scrap-yards. Stanley Topliss and a pal came across a great quantity of gliders stored in a field at Fall Lane, Sowerby Bridge, and they were soon the proud possessors of such items as compasses and altimeters. Geoff Whiteley, at the end of the war, witnessed the incongruous sight at Shackleton's scrap-yard, Siddal, of children playing in aeroplanes that might once have witnessed heroics. Colin Wakefield saw Spitfires and Lancasters at Charlie Holmes' scrap-yard, and it was known that the yard paid £50 for a Spitfire. It was perhaps a little sad to see such fine aircraft so quickly consigned to history, but they had played out their part, and the time for the local souvenir collectors had come.

NOT HURTING LORD WOOLTON'S FEELINGS

'Those who have the will to win,
Cook potatoes in their skin,
Knowing that the sight of peelings
Deeply hurts Lord Woolton's feelings.'

Lord Woolton, Minister of Food from April 1940 to November 1942, would have fully approved of having his name linked to this little jingle, for it summed up the qualities that the British people would be required to show if the war on the Home Front was to be pursued successfully – determination, healthy eating, avoidance of waste, and the consumption of seemingly endless quantities of potatoes. Also, if one feature of everyday war time life was to brand itself indelibly into the memories of that generation, particularly housewives, it was rationing and all that was associated with it – scarcity, long queues, 'making do' and the most reasonable request to a shopkeeper frequently provoking the outraged response of, "Don't you know there's a war on?"

A recipe which just had to be popular with Lord Woolton.

Britain was heavily reliant on imported food and it was clear from the start that, just as in World War One, a key German strategy would be to starve Britain into surrender by means of 'U'-boat attacks on merchant ships carrying that food. Even in 1939, almost 200,000 tons of shipping was sunk monthly, a figure that was to peak at almost 600,000 tons in the black month of April 1941. In addition, so many industries at home were being transformed into 'war industries' at the expense of 'non-essential' items that the supply of consumer goods was down by about 75% in November 1941 as compared to September 1939. Therefore rationing was an inevitability. The question was, when? Perhaps surprisingly, the first Christmas of the war, that of 1939, was an unrationed one, although shortages were already being felt. It was not until 1940, however, that the screw began to be turned and, month by month, rationing began to ease its way in. People could see a hard road ahead, but little did they know how long that road would be. Who, for example, would ever have dreamed that bacon, first rationed in January 1940, would remain so until July 1954?

On September 29th 1939 the entire nation had been 'registered' in a process somewhat like a census. On the basis of the information gathered, identity cards had been issued, along with the first ration books – buff coloured for general use and blue (later green) for children under six years. Expectant mothers also had green ration books. On January 8th 1940, the first food items were put under control – bacon, butter and sugar. Over the next nineteen months, controls were extended to tea, margarine and lard, jam and marmalade, cheese, eggs and milk. The weekly amounts allowed per person tended to vary during the course of the war. The following table gives some examples. To work out modern equivalents, it needs to be remembered that 4 ounces (oz) equals 114 grammes, and that there are 16 ounces in one pound (lb).

Meat was rationed in a slightly different way in that an adult could buy almost two shillings worth (10p) per week in March 1940,

Food	Least Allowed	Most Allowed
Bacon	4oz	8oz
Cheese	1oz	8oz
Sugar	8oz	16oz **
Tea	2oz	4oz
Butter	2oz	4oz
Fat	1oz	8oz
Eggs	half	2
(plus extra for jam making)**		

and this amount of money could buy around one and a half pounds of beef, pork or mutton; sausages were not on the controlled list. This was not a bad amount, but availability was another matter and, in any case, by 1942 the meat ration had been virtually halved. Offal was not rationed, nor were poultry, game or fish. These tended to go up in price and disappear 'under the counter.'

Matters took a turn for the worse in July 1942, especially for children, when confectionery (basically chocolate and sweets) was rationed at 2 oz per week, although this was soon raised to 3 oz. The milk ration worked out at around 3 pints per person weekly, and by this time even bread had fallen victim to stringent regulation. February 1941 saw the introduction of the famous National Wheatmeal Bread, with only 15% of the wheat discarded as chaff. The result was a rather grey coloured and coarse textured bread, healthier but not very popular. Bread was not rationed, but by April 1942 the sale of the more refined white loaf was made illegal.

Bread matters were taken very seriously, and it was advised that spare bread was not to be fed to the birds, but was to be crushed into crumbs for cooking. In June 1943, a Halifax woman was fined for the offence of 'wasting bread.'

Attempts were made to build flexibility into the system where special needs were seen. Expectant and nursing mothers were allowed a pint of subsidised milk per day, as were adolescents and invalids. The mothers and mothers-to-be also received concentrated orange juice, cod liver oil and vitamin supplements, plus extra egg and meat rations.

Manual workers such as miners and farm hands enjoyed an extra cheese allowance. From December 1941 all adults had sixteen 'points' per month added to their ration books with which they would be able to buy canned foods – meat, fish, fruit, milk etc – and packaged

"Queuing became a way of life."

foods, wherever they could find them. Shoppers could trawl around in search of extras, without having to be restricted to the retailers they were registered with.

The great British public reacted with typical stoicism. Queuing became a way of life for housewives looking for that little bit extra, hoping that if anything had gone 'under the counter' they might be among the favoured ones. A housewife might join a queue without any clear idea of what was being queued for, just in the hope that there might be something worth the wait at the end of it. It might have turned out to be horsemeat, or worse still whalemeat. Harold and Mary Doyle of Gibbet Street, found horsemeat tolerable, but not

FOOD FACTS

Meet the new fish

Strange new fish on the fish-monger's slab — fish you've never met before, but well worth knowing all the same.

You get these new fish because of the zoning scheme: fish is now sold close to where it is landed instead of being sent far journeys to its old markets.

There are two kinds of strangers, *round white fish* (cousins of the cod), and *flat fish*. It it well worth while to look out for them in case they come your way. And don't judge them by their outlandish names or unfamiliar looks—beauty in a fish isn't skin deep!

These newcomers have a fine flavour, are an economical food and are quick and easy to cook.

No mention here of the dreaded Snoek.

whalemeat. The latter tended to be grey in colour, oily and strongly flavoured in taste. A brand of tinned fish came on the market which seemed to belong to no known species of fish. Even its name was unfortunate – 'Snoek' – and to quote a Calderdale resident at the time, "It smelled revolting." Even her cat retreated from it in disgust.

The bright yellow dried egg powder which began to arrive from the USA in June 1942 may not have been appreciated for its colour, but the one packet per month allowed on each adult ration book (more for children) certainly helped out with the baking. Similarly, each family could have one tin of dried skimmed milk powder per month. With water added, it was said to be the equivalent of four pints of liquid milk. Goods had begun to flow from the USA, under the Lend-Lease Scheme, as early as March 1940, and under the 'points' system Spam (Supply Pressed American Meat) and Mor (sweetened ham) became popular buys. By common consent, the best buy for the whole of the sixteen 'points' was a large tin of American sausage meat. It provided enough meat for several main meals, and the thick layer of fat at the top was excellent for cooking purposes.

YOU ARE ALLOWED I PACKET OF DRIED EGGS PER RATION BOOK EVERY 4 WEEKS (2 FOR GREEN BOOKS)
LISTEN TO THE KITCHEN FRONT EVERY MORNING AT 8.15
ISSUED BY THE MINISTRY OF FOOD; LONDON, W.I.   FOOD FACTS No. 167

The bright yellow dried egg powder from the USA certainly came in useful.

> *Rationing affected people in unexpected ways. Dennis Greenwood's father, living at Kebroyd in the Ryburn Valley, was a keen breeder and keeper of budgerigars. From very early on in the war, he could get no food for them. His hobby literally flew out of the window as he simply had to let his fifty or so 'budgies' go. They did not last more than a few months in the harsh outside world, and it must have been a sorrowful sight to see their numbers diminishing in the nearby woods.*

A Sowerby Bridge pigeon fancier found that his hobby was not at all affected by rationing. Pigeons were used by many aircraft, ships and army units as message carriers. They were also regarded as being of potential use in the event of telephone links being put out of action during an invasion. The local pigeon fancier volunteered to breed and supply birds to the National Pigeon Service. He also had to remain 'on alert' to be sent to any loft, at home or abroad. He was never called upon to do this, and for his services he was allowed 28 lbs of corn for every pigeon he supplied, along with exemption from Home Guard duty. As for those birds of another feather – hens – one could substitute the egg ration for chicken meal and have a go at hen keeping which, with luck, provided a greater supply of eggs.

By and large, rationing was felt by the public to be the only fair system. In a time of scarcity, the only alternative would have been to let

---

"pineapples at 5 guineas (£5.25p) each."

---

prices find their own level, meaning plenty for the 'haves' and little or nothing for the 'have nots.' As it was, rationing was accompanied by retail price control. Fresh fruit was uncontrolled in this respect, and an example of what might have happened without controls elsewhere was seen in London in September 1944 – pineapples at 5 guineas (£5.25p) each. People were quick to latch on if they felt that a retailer was exceeding a controlled price. In February 1941, after complaints from a customer, a Luddenden Foot grocer was fined for selling tinned milk, damson jam and raspberry jam at above the controlled price. His argument was that it was impossible to keep up with the flow of constantly changing prices from the Ministry of Food.

Whilst accepting the rationing regime, most people didn't mind a little bending of the regulations if they felt that nobody was being exploited. They would have regarded the 'black market' as too strong a term for what they were engaged in, which generally involved the humble pig as a co-conspirator. It might be said, at least as far as Halifax and Calderdale were concerned, that during the war years the pig replaced the dog as man's best friend. The district witnessed a growing traffic in mysterious parcels during these years, especially at Christmas. Colin Wakefield made

---

"the pig replaced the dog as man's best friend."

---

more than one journey by bus as a boy from his home in Lee Mount to a house in Greetland. Money would be exchanged; a parcel slipped into his paper carrier bag; no questions asked. Dennis Greenwood's father, a milkman with good farming contacts, once sent him with a personal delivery to a police sergeant of their acquaintance. A lady living in the Savile Park area had a similarly obliging milkman who, from time to time, would silently slip down the cellar steps and leave a little parcel there. And the common denominator in all this? Pork.

Had all this been known to the Ministry of Food, it would have caused great displeasure and, no doubt, fines. It wasn't that the government itself was not keen on pigs. It encouraged Pig Clubs in urban areas and had huge bins set up so that kitchen waste could be processed and dispatched to hungry pigs. It was just that anyone who reared pigs could slaughter just one per year for their own consumption, and the rest had to be declared to the Ministry and enter the rationing system. In a semi-rural area such as this, no one was too far from a farm or contact with a milkman/farmer, and illicit pig killings were commonplace. That the local law enforcement

agencies turned a blind eye to it is putting it mildly. Keith Newbitt's family, who lived at Birchcliffe in Hebden Bridge, always looked forward to its regular Christmas piece of pork provided by the milkman, who also farmed at Wadsworth. Unfortunately, news leaked out one Christmas that an undeclared pig was being fattened up for killing, and some disgruntled person not on the favoured list 'shopped' the milkman to the police. The local constable sent

The humble pig – now man's best friend.

to investigate duly made all the arrangements for the confiscation of the pig, and then gave the culprit a good dressing down, not so much for the offence as for not keeping it more of a secret. Not only would the Newbitt family have to do without its pork at the festive season, but so would the constable, for he too had been on the list.

Another Christmas; another place. In Todmorden a butcher is busy at his premises in the centre of town late at night. All is quiet as straining their ears in the kitchen, soon became aware that a sharing out of 'black' pork was going on. The identity of the conspirators was blown wide open by the fact that the leader had a stutter, and as he laboriously read out all the names on the parcels, and handed them out, his voice came loudly through the thin walls. Finally, with every parcel gone, Doreen's father said, "Bert, where's the one for Road Studs?" The reply was uncompromising. "B-b-bugger Road Studs Albert, he wouldn't think about us." So 'Road Studs,' in spite of his services to humanity, was left out of that particular carve-up!

The Newbitt family – had to do without its Christmas crackling.

he makes up his 'black' orders, safe from observation behind his very legitimate blacked-out windows. Suddenly the door rattles as heavy knocks reverberate around his little shop. He freezes. Is it the men from the Ministry? He stays dead quiet as further knocks come. Gradually the knocking dies away, but he remains still and silent. After a couple of hours he decides that the coast must be clear. Stealthily opening the door, he slips out with his orders and turns to lock up. To his horror two policeman loom up out of the darkness, one on each side of him. "What's tha kept us so long for Binny? Chief told us to pick up his meat, and happen tha's got a bit spare for us." Sighs of relief from Binny!

The elaborate deceptions involved in illicit pig killing around the district were probably enjoyed for the thrill of the conspiracy element as much as anything else. Hence, one winter's evening, Doreen Russell and her mother were hustled out of the front room of their house at Siddal when the noise of a taxi drawing up outside was heard. Visitors came clumping into the front room. Doreen and her mother,

The men from the Ministry of Food were prone to making unannounced, but perhaps not random visits. They knew what they were looking for, but did not always find it. One advantage of living on a farm was that visitors could usually be spotted at a distance, and in the case of a Blackshaw Head farmer he was able to pack his wife off to bed with a supposed illness before the inspector arrived at the door. Nevertheless, he popped his head around the bedroom door to offer his best wishes for a speedy recovery, little knowing that she was fondly nursing a couple of large hams under the bedsheets.

The government had its own agenda for coping with shortages of imported food, and high on this agenda was the desire for the country to grow much more of its own food. As early as October 1939, the 'Fight the Submarines with Spades' slogan was aired. Then the famous 'Dig for Victory' campaign was launched – an inspired slogan that endured long after the war had ended. The entire population was urged to turn its gardens into vegetable plots, with the great national gardening expert, Mr Middleton, always on hand to dispense advise via the wireless set. The Minister of Education suggested that all schools should cultivate vegetables, especially potatoes. Philip Hanson, a pupil at Christ Church School, Pellon, was amazed at the rapidity with which shops emptied themselves of items such as apples, onions and soap, and

One of the iconic images of the Home Front.

Government ambitions went wider than this. Farmers had to plough a proportion of their land under Ministry instructions, usually for potatoes or swedes locally. Public parks were ploughed up. Eric Thomas, a boy living at Todmorden in these years, was amazed to see Centre Vale Park ploughed up and turned into allotments. The same astonishment was felt in Halifax in 1942, as Savile Park suffered the same fate, but this was just another reality of life on the Home Front – 'the world turned upside down.' The government was very anxious to foster the right public attitudes and it provided free seeds and fertilisers to new allotment holders. Helpful tips and advice, both about growing food and how to make best use of it, poured from the wireless. Lord Woolton, Minister of Food, gave a short talk entitled, 'The Kitchen Front' (a handy fighting metaphor) every morning. He promoted short 'Food Flashes' on the cinema screen. He himself was greatly admired; his famous Woolton Pie less so. Needless to say it was entirely composed of vegetables.

how quickly butchers' shops reduced their opening times to sometimes as little as two days per week. He was one of those who found that Gardening had entered the school timetable in 1940, but seemingly for the boys only, who were equipped with clogs, spades and rakes, and set to turning over a field in Pellon. The eventual produce was sold at school. Advice from the Ministry also included the mechanics of setting up school Rabbit Clubs, although it is likely

An amazing sight – Savile Park under the plough.

Courtesy of Stephen Gee

that some difficulties were encountered when the younger children realised that their beloved pets were about to become ingredients in a stew. In this respect, the government lifted all restrictions on keeping poultry and rabbits in domestic gardens.

Other favourite characters on the five minute 'Kitchen Front' programme were comediennes Gert and Daisy (fictional charladies) and the 'Radio Doctor,' Charles Hill. Gert and Daisy even produced their own 'Wartime Cookery Book,' full of tantalising recipes.

The meat recommended was usually offal – not rationed but still scarce, and often only obtainable from 'under the counter.' People had to use their imaginations to provide the meat content for the all-vegetable mock chicken cutlets, and it required real inventiveness to persuade children that sweet potato chocolate spread had anything to do with chocolate at all. The 'Patsy' newspaper cartoon strip specialised in concocting palatable meals from the most humble ingredients. Cooking any sort of food provided a problem in itself as fat was on ration. Liquid paraffin offered an alternative, as did whale oil. Perhaps it was as well not to know that Neatsfoot Oil was made from animal hooves, although the smell of glue that accompanied the cooking might well have given the game away.

> *Who could possibly have resisted some of the wartime delicacies promoted by the government – sheep's brains on toast with acorn coffee, for example, or stewed ox cheek?*

Above all, the virtues of vegetables were extolled in government propaganda, especially potatoes. Lord Woolton was notoriously fond of them, and must have been gratified that their consumption went up by 60% during the war.

MISS LIGHTFOOT works in a factory all day. She makes no song or dance about it, but she is doing her bit. And the thing you couldn't help noticing is that even in wartime conditions she is seldom tired, never ill, never nervy. What is it Miss Lightfoot does that perhaps you don't? She eats potatoes and carrots. So do you. But *she* eats them every day—and every day in a different way. They protect her from illness and fatigue and keep her full of vitality. They'll do just the same for you.

Potatoes and carrots – cured all ills.

Cartoon characters such as Potato Pete and Doctor Carrot were created, especially for children, and it was suggested that it was more patriotic to eat home-grown potatoes than bread because most wheat supplies had to be imported. It was useful also to imply that carrots had a mysterious and almost magical quality that enabled those who ate them to see better in the dark, a great bonus during the 'blackout.' Carrots were credited with enabling the RAF pilot, 'Cat's Eyes' Cunningham, to shoot down many enemy planes at night. Radar was conveniently not mentioned. Carrots more seriously could be used as a sweetener, and the war saw the advent of carrot cake.

National efforts to educate the public were reinforced at a local level. September 1941 saw Halifax 'Food Week,' which 'kicked off' with a communal meal for 200 guests at the Gibbet Street Institute, and an address by the wife of Halifax MP Gilbert Gledhill. During the week, Ministry of Food representatives were able to use the gas and electricity showrooms as food advice bureaux. Pamphlets were handed out which gave tips on salad and jam making, and how best to store vegetables. The Halifax 'Dig

"Food is a munition of war. Don't waste it."

For Victory' campaign of March 1943 followed similar lines, with the additions of exhibitions on gardening techniques, including food preservation methods, and lectures on keeping bees and rabbits. In the eyes of Lord Woolton, another crucial element in educating the public was the avoidance of waste. "Food is a munition of war. Don't waste it." If his feelings were to be hurt by people peeling their potatoes before cooking them, and thus missing out on the nutritional value of the skins, then the least they could do was to make sure that the peelings went to the pigs. Local councils set up huge pig-bins on the streets into which virtually all kitchen food waste could be placed. 'Rubbish Makes Rashers' was the government slogan. Pigs were not quite as undiscriminating as goats, for people were not to include rhubarb leaves, tea leaves or coffee grounds.

BETTER POT-LUCK

with Churchill today

THAN HUMBLE PIE

under Hitler tomorrow

DON'T WASTE FOOD!

A very clever piece of government propaganda.

As a boy, Colin Wakefield was very impressed by the huge modified Lancashire boiler into which the contents of the collected pig bins were discharged, along with refuse from the borough market and abattoir. This steam-heated monster which the cleansing department had set up on Charlestown Road, Halifax, contained a big worm which rendered the waste down into appetising food for pigs. Local farmers collected the resultant 'swill,' whilst allotment owners could collect bonemeal from bones ground up on the same site.

The government did its best in difficult circumstances. By 1944, land under the plough had increased by 50% and pastureland by 66%. As a result the output of wheat and barley had almost doubled, and the quantity of potatoes produced had more than doubled. Food was subsidised (by almost £206 million in 1943) so that food prices were kept within 20% of the pre-war level. Nevertheless people could not help but mourn the almost total disappearance of imported fruit from the shelves. Bananas and oranges became things of fond memory. There

was no need for price control; they were simply not there.

> *Home grown vegetables were plentiful; imported ones were a different matter. French and Spanish onions virtually vanished. In February 1941 a 1.5 lb onion was raffled among the staff of 'The Times' and it raised £4 3s 4d (£4.17p).*

Were there any ways to beat the strictures of rationing other than dabbling in the 'black market?' One way was a return to barter, sometimes in the form of an exchange of skills for goods. In most cases, a dozen eggs or a chicken was preferable to cash for any job done for a farmer. Goods for goods were not an unusual transaction, as in the case of the local girl who received a lipstick allowance through her work at a chemists. She was happy to swap some of this for that rarity, oranges, with a grocer who wanted to keep his wife happy.

The government had its own ideas about how people might legitimately ease the burden of rationing, and in December 1941 Halifax's civic leaders were the first in the locality to sample the fare at the town's first British Restaurant, situated in the lower market. An appetising three course meal was served, consisting of celery soup, followed by roast beef, potatoes and Brussels sprouts, topped off with sponge pudding and custard, and a cup of tea – all for 11d (4.5p). Officially opening the restaurant the Mayor, Alderman Percival

Checking out the menu at the British Restaurant, Heptonstall.

Courtesy of the Longstaff Collection

Whitley, stressed not only the good value for money aspect of the meals being served, but also the economies of bulk cooking as opposed to hundreds of meals being prepared individually at home.

> *The idea of British Restaurants arose from the setting up of static communal feeding centres to cater for those who were being badly affected in 'blitzed' areas. The government extended them, under the name of British Restaurants, across the country. From the 246 in existence in 119 towns in April 1941, the number had grown to 1000 by the August of that year.*

Not only did British Restaurants offer the advantages outlined by the Mayor of Halifax, but they allowed the multitude of war workers the chance to get a nutritious meal quickly, thus lessening the disruption to the working day. In fact British Restaurants also soon developed a busy takeaway system, providing 'out' deliveries to factories. The Halifax eating house was able to provide 500 meals per day on the premises, as well as the takeaway service, and a second British Restaurant for Halifax was to open at Stoney Royd in July 1942. However, Heptonstall led the field in this respect, the first British Restaurant in the locality having being opened in the Church School there in June 1941. Todmorden had no less than five, the first one opening in September 1941.

At the other end of the Calder Valley, British Restaurants opened their doors at Park Row, Brighouse and at Rastrick New Road Sunday School. The Lightcliffe Liberal Club, later to become the Lightcliffe Preparatory School, contained a British Restaurant upstairs. The long queues reported at similar establishments at Hebden Bridge and Mytholmroyd in August 1942 is a testament to their popularity. However, by the end of March 1944 both these British Restaurants had closed, along with many others in the area. Therefore it must be assumed that either the government felt that the need for them had passed, or that their popularity had waned.

It is difficult to believe that an institution as mundane and straightforward as a British Restaurant could be open to a mild 'racket,' but three bright young sparks managed to dream one up. Kathleen Heys joined the Naval Victualling Department of the Admiralty in Halifax as an office junior, in 1943. Her fellow

> *"this junior 'mafia' soon built up jam jars full of tokens"*

office juniors, Margery and Margaret, were both aged 14 in 1943, as was Kathleen herself, and as such were entitled to free lunch vouchers at a British Restaurant. A daily voucher could be exchanged at the cash desk for different coloured tokens, one for each course. With the restaurant at Halifax lower market as their favoured location, this junior 'mafia' soon built up jam jars full of tokens by missing a course here and a course there. These they would sell to older colleagues at work – at a cut price of course. This nice little sideline came to an abrupt halt when the restaurant did a few calculations and informed 'high command' at the Naval Victualling Department. The girls were hauled up before their boss, and may have been expecting to be 'clapped in irons,' but escaped with a fairly mild reprimand.

Rationing on the whole was a success for the government. The general public accepted the necessity for it and its overall fairness, whilst tolerating the inescapable fact that those with money could gain an advantage through the 'black market.' One unexpected bonus was an improvement in the health of the nation, brought about by the drastic reduction in fat and sugar in the everyday diet, accompanied by a corresponding increase in the consumption of vegetables. Even the lack of fresh fruit did not overcome this advance. Another simple factor was that people had to do more walking in their day-to-day living. The government slogan, 'Use Shank's Pony – walk when you can,' was more a recognition of what people were having to do rather than inviting them to make a conscious decision. The 9 pm bus curfew in Halifax, and a train network dominated by military needs, saw to that. On the other hand, walking was good for the health.

FOOD FACTS

Thank the farmer – bless the weather –

for plenty of green vegetables *NOW!*

A mild season has advanced the crops—that's **why** health-giving green vegetables are top-of-the-bill this week. Make the most of them while they last! We all need all the Vitamin C we can get, *and* more variety in our diet. Make cabbage a "special" tonight. Make greenstuffs a daily "extra" while they stay plentiful and cheap. It's nothing but common sense to go for the good things while they are at their cheapest and most abundant. So fill up your shopping basket at the greengrocer's!

Then as now, "Eat up your greens!"

In particular, the special attention paid to expectant and nursing mothers meant a fall in the infant mortality rate in the United Kingdom to an all time low in 1943. Even more strikingly, the maternal death rate in childbirth in 1944 was just above one half of the 1938 level. Wartime factory workers endured long hours, but often there were more in the way of nurses and welfare workers then there had ever been before. There is little doubt, however, that wartime children on the Home Front would have sacrificed all these gains for the great lack in their lives – sweets. Could the 21st Century child even imagine it – at its worst a ration of 2 oz (57 grammes) per week – the equivalent of a medium sized chocolate bar? Unless parents or other relatives came good with their sweet ration coupons, that was it.

A blending of cocoa, syrup and dried milk boiled up, could create a very acceptable type

The search for sweet substitutes was a never-ending one for children. Raw carrot sliced up in jelly could almost be classed as 'sweets.' A closer equivalent to the real thing could be conjured up out of cocoa. There was real excitement amongst the pupils at Holy Trinity School, Savile Park, when it became known that a consignment of cocoa powder had arrived there from the USA. Jean Fields was one of the many to take a jam jar into school to get a share of this treat.

of sweet. Meanwhile in Hebden Bridge, John Tolley's recipe was a little less sophisticated – a raw mixture of cocoa, sugar and oatmeal with one or more grubby, wet fingers constantly dipping into it. Once again it was the cocoa which came to the rescue of a number of Sowerby Bridge children. They were able to collect syrup drippings in jam jars from the tankers that made deliveries to Mattock's Sweet Factory. Mixed with cocoa, these drippings produced something which at least resembled a sweet.

To the modern eye, the rationing of food with the seemingly miserly quantities allowed of such basic items as butter and bacon, seems a tale of miserable hardship. It was hard enough. Even in a semi-rural area like our own, a rabbit for the stewpot was a rare treat. However, it is a mistake to view these wartime years from the perspective of 21st Century supermarket shelves bulging with every imaginable variety of food, and people with money in their pockets to buy it. The war came hard on the heels of the 'hungry thirties,' a decade of high unemployment and depressed wages. For working class people, the contrast between what they could buy under rationing, and what they had been able to buy before, was not so great as it would be today. Sadly, for the poorest section of society, rationing made scarcely any difference at all. Coupons did not buy food; money had to accompany the coupons. This was the problem. The 2 oz sweet ration was no hardship to the child who did not have the money to buy sweets anyway, and to whom sweets had been an unattainable luxury before the war. In such cases coupons remained unused, or even sold, a scenario that was even more prevalent when it came to clothing.

"WOT NO ꝺ ANYTHING?"

Chad may never really have draped his long nose over the wall and said, "Wot No Bombs?" in the early months of the war, but he was to come into his own as rationing began to bite from 1940. In cartoon form, he was able to express the muted voice of public complaint about the lack of bananas, pleats in skirts, coal, petrol, furniture, candles, crockery – in fact, just about anything except potatoes and carrots. Second only to food, the acquisition of clothing probably caused most difficulties for those on the Home Front after clothes had entered the rationing system in June 1941, along with textiles. Each adult was allocated 66 coupons per year for clothing, (reduced to 48 in 1942) with extra points for children, babies and expectant mothers. It was a matter then of juggling the coupons to stretch them throughout the year, for whereas a boy's vest only required two coupons, a suit or a coat or a dress could need anything from ten to sixteen coupons.

The government took a more direct hand here by introducing 'Utility Clothes,' made under the direction of the Board of Trade. These were manufactured from a limited range of materials, but they were of good quality and hardwearing. 'Utility' clothing was quite stylish, if a little severe, for it was decidedly lacking in frills – no double-breasted coats or turn-ups for men; no embroidery or trimmings on women's clothes, along with limited pleats and buttons. Prices were controlled, and the famous 'Utility' label made its appearance – 'CC41' (Civilian Clothing 1941). The 'Utility' scheme proved successful enough to be extended to pottery, cooking utensils, suitcases, umbrellas, cutlery and household textiles. Also, from January 1943, all new items of

HAIGHS MARKET STREET, HEBDEN BRIDGE

Fashion to the fore - even with coupon restrictions.

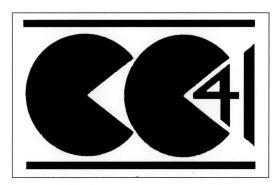

The 'Utility' mark – Civilian Clothing 1941: a guarantee of value.

furniture had to bear the 'Utility' stamp, and once again it was plain and functional, but very soundly constructed. It was regarded as good value for money and, as such, was very popular. An allocation system based on need was put in place, as opposed to ration coupons, and the priorities included newly-weds and those who had been bombed out. Neither the Board of Trade nor anyone else could have anticipated that controls on furniture would not be lifted until 1952.

As with food, the effects of rationing on other commodities were entirely dependent upon circumstances. For some the struggle was to get enough with the coupons; for others the problem was the money, and the coupons were virtually irrelevant. Dora Longbottom, living on Wakefield Road, Copley, was one of the latter. Her husband was a prisoner of the Japanese, and she was left with her meagre serviceman's allowance to bring up two young children and, for some time, an evacuee from London. Shortage of money meant that she used very few of her clothing coupons. She was the very epitome of the 'Make Do and Mend' philosophy which the government was trying to promote, but which in any case was not too far removed from the necessities of working class life in pre-war days. That Dora was very adept

---

"as the war lengthened, Dora's brush and shovel shortened"

---

at coping with bedsheets which had worn in the middle was perhaps a product of long practice. She slit them down the middle, 'turned them' so that the less worn outer parts now formed the middle, and sewed them together again. She cut her own clothes down to make garments for her children. When her shovel turned up at the end, she cut a bit off. She did the same with her hand brush as the bristles wore away at the end. And so, as the war lengthened, Dora's brush and shovel shortened. If the war had gone on much longer....

Marjorie Brierley was in a similar position to Dora Longbottom. Living on Gibbet Street, with her husband away in the Pioneer Corps

and having to survive on a services allowance of 25 shillings (£1.25) per week for herself and her baby, she too found that clothing coupons were a little academic. Ingenuity was the key, and Marjorie managed to make shirts out of cotton sugar bags for her son. With the general

The date shows that rationing did not end with the war.

shortage of household linen – sheets, curtains, towels etc. – sugar bags might also become curtains, as did butter muslin from time to time. Flour sacks were bleached or dyed to be transformed into sheets or tablecloths. In their turn, old curtains could reappear as dresses, but the most sought after commodity in this respect was parachute silk. This was, of course, relatively rare and it was out of 'bits and pieces' that Alice Beaumont, in Hebden Bridge, managed to put together a siren suit for her young daughter Diane.

> *The Newbitt family, of Hebden Bridge, showed self-help of a high order. Young Roy bred rabbits and both he and his cousin, Keith, marvelled at what grandma could do with the skins, curing them and making not only mittens, but also a coat.*

Mary Crossley, living at Oak Terrace, off Hanson Lane, also made many of her own clothes at this time but, as always, it paid to have friends in the right places. She received plenty of clothing coupons from a wealthy friend who bought them from people who could not afford to use them.

The government was keener on the 'Make Do and Mend' aspect of self-help as opposed to dealings in clothing coupons. In this respect, the rather curious rag-doll figure of 'Mrs Sew-and-Sew' appeared on leaflets and posters, giving out tips and hints, such as invisible mending for laddered nylons. Self-help classes

'Mrs Sew-and-Sew' to the rescue again.

mushroomed under local authority provision. Aimed at the female population, they provided for a pooling of ideas as well as the opportunity for some socialising. Some of the more unlikely ideas included the making of

necklaces from old buttons, and a handbag from knotted string. Exhibitions played their part too, and one was arranged at the Electricity

---

"re-heeling stockings from cast-off stocking legs."

Board Showrooms by Mrs Parsons, Head of the Women's Work Department of the Halifax Technical College. The theme was the creation of, "garments and wearing apparel made from old clothes that have become demoded." It was shown how, for example, an old Ulster cape had been re-invented as a dressing gown. At a simpler level, women visitors apparently showed keen interest in the technique of re-heeling stockings from cast-off stocking legs.

Unravelling and unpicking old woollen garments in order to knit new ones became a popular pastime, especially as knitting wool had joined the lengthening ration list. Knitting and sewing circles thrived, and the Women's Voluntary Service was prominent in efforts to knit socks, gloves and balaclavas for the forces. Knitted items probably made up a large proportion of the parcels put together by the Halifax Comforts Fund at its centre in Crossley Street. It is remarkable that during a time of deprivation at home, the volunteers of the Halifax Comforts Fund were able to send out a stream of parcels to local service personnel at home and abroad, and to prisoners-of-war. Between January 1942 and January 1943, for example, more than 15,000 parcels were dispatched to the forces. Just over 10,000 Halifax servicemen and servicewomen were on the fund's register at the end of 1942, and exactly 235 prisoners or civilian internees. This latter total of 235 included a reported 54 prisoners of the Japanese, but it was not possible at this stage to send parcels to those in the Far East.

"Use no more than five inches of water in your bath."

'Making do' applied also to keeping clean during these shortage years. Not only was soap rationed, but one of the more unwelcome government exhortations was to, "Use no more than five inches of water in your bath." It has to be admitted that in those days bathing was more of a weekly than a daily ritual for many people. Nevertheless, whether in a tin bath before the fire, or in a well-appointed bathroom, it was a much less pleasant experience with the water at around twelve centimetres, barely above the knees. This was not really a water saving measure. The thinking behind the government's campaign was to save fuel in the heating of the water. It was very difficult to ration gas or electricity. As for coal, it was simply in scarce supply and difficult to get hold of. Government advice even extended

Cold comfort rather than 'coal comfort' in these austere years.

to dissolving a tablespoon of salt in half a pint of water and sprinkling it over the coal, which was supposed to make it burn more slowly.

By 1944 coal consumption was down nationally by 25% as compared to 1938, and so freezing homes became another disincentive to having the 'luxury' five inches soak in the bath.

People were sometimes reduced to scavenging around for anything to burn, including old furniture and shoes.

Coke was one fuel option, but not much of one in the eyes of young Doreen Russell, living in Siddal. She hated the occasions when she and her mother made the trip to Elland Power Station, where they were allowed two pennyworth of coke. This was transported home on Doreen's sledge, and though they were 'keeping the home fires burning,' she felt it was much beneath her dignity.

Bedtime in an ice-cold home was as big an ordeal as bathtime, for incredibly enough, hot-water bottles could only be got on prescription. A hot oven plate wrapped in flannel sometimes served to warm up the bedsheets a little, or even a hot brick in a towel.

If the acquisition of coal became a problem for the many, then shortages of another type of fuel – petrol – provided a headache for only a few. The 1940s was not the age of the motorcar, although there were plenty of motorcycles about. At a very early date indeed, September 16th 1939, in anticipation of scarcity, price controls were put on petrol. The maximum price was fixed at a level which, by modern standards, would appear to be absolutely mouth-watering – 1s 6d (7.5p) per gallon. Petrol then became the first commodity to be rationed, only a week later. Motorists were allowed from 4 gallons per month for the likes of an Austin Seven, up to 10 gallons per month for a car of 20-horse power or more. This ration provided enough for between 100 and 200 miles of motoring. There was a good deal of heart searching, however, as to whether seamen's lives should continue to be put at risk for what was, after all, a luxury. From March 1942 no basic ration was provided for private motoring, which was now banned.

The problems of wartime motoring before the ban were such that the ban itself might have come as something of a relief. The petrol ration did not go far. As always, the 'black market'

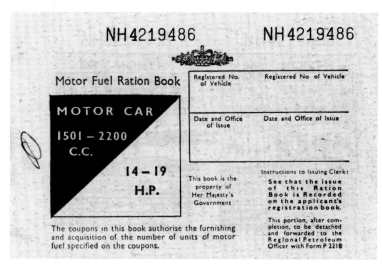

NH 4219486   NH 4219486

Motor Fuel Ration Book

MOTOR CAR
1501 – 2200
C.C.

14 – 19
H.P.

Registered No. of Vehicle

Date and Office of Issue

This book is the property of Her Majesty's Government

Registered No of Vehicle

Date and Office of Issue

Instructions to Issuing Clerk:
See that the issue of this Ration Book is Recorded on the applicant's registration book.

This portion, after completion, to be detached and forwarded to the Regional Petroleum Officer with Form P 2218

The coupons in this book authorise the furnishing and acquisition of the number of units of motor fuel specified on the coupons.

The meagre fuel ration soon disappeared altogether for private motorists.

offered extra supplies, but at a price that was more eye-watering than mouth-watering – around six shillings (30p) a gallon. Much of the illegal petrol had been literally siphoned away from stocks earmarked for commercial use only. It was dyed red for easy identification, but it was soon found that the colour could be removed by pouring petrol through a gas mask filter. This might not have been the end of the matter, however, for apparently the police could still detect illegal petrol by placing paper over the end of an exhaust pipe and checking the colour of the fumes.

"'Heath Robinson' type contraption on the roof of the car"

Another short-lived but legal way to get around petrol rationing was to adapt a car to run on household gas. This involved a 'Heath Robinson' type contraption on the roof of the car – a wooden cradle supporting a huge gas-filled balloon. This sight both amused and amazed pedestrians, but it was never very practical as the balloon only held the equivalent of one gallon of petrol. The experiment was continued on buses after the ban on private motoring, but the buses had to tow coal-

burning apparatus on small trailers to keep the gas supply going to the balloons.

During the first two years of the war, the spy mania was at its height, and so motoring became troublesome for another reason. To lock up a car at night was no longer enough. By law a motorist had also to take off the rotor arm in the engine in case any roaming spies might try to steal the car, an emergency measure that was not relaxed until June 1943. A letter to the 'Hebden Bridge Times' in June 1941, sent by a national cycling organisation, advised cyclists to remove the pedals of their machines at night. After March 1942, however, for the

PARK MOTORS (HX.) LTD.

PORTLAND PLACE, HALIFAX.   Tel. 4791/92.

DISTRIBUTORS FOR : ROVER CARS, HUMBER CARS, MORRIS CARS AND MORRIS (NEW MODEL) VANS.

Also a big stock of Second Hand MORRIS Cars.

Series II. 8 h.p.   Series I. 8 h.p.

Series II. 10/4.   Series II. 18 h.p.

This 1940 advertisement was virtually redundant by 1942.

motorists at least, it was all over. Even vehicle sales were prohibited except under special licence. The car went 'into mothballs.' At Todmorden, Vincent Holt's father, William Holt, put the car up on blocks, and it was Vincent's task occasionally to crank the engine up with the starting handle to keep the forlorn vehicle in some type of running order.

After the banning of private motoring, the government slogan of, 'Is Your Journey Really Necessary?' took on a sharper edge. The police could stop any vehicle and ask for 'proof of need.' Petrol was still available for those who needed an allowance for business or professional reasons, such as farmers, factory owners or doctors. However, the armed forces were in dire need of petrol and to use it illegally was deemed to be unpatriotic. As a result, the courts showed little sympathy. As early as February 1940, three Halifax men were fined the considerable sum of £40 for illegal storage of petrol, considered to be 'hoarding.' There were many complaints in the newspapers about the numbers of cars still to be seen at race meetings. Nothing seemed to be done about this, but it was not in the government's interests for it to be thought that the wealthy or influential could always get away with it. In 1944 a well-known actor and composer was imprisoned for a month for abusing the system.

> *A Triangle bus driver could count himself as being unfortunate in June 1943. Having missed the bus that would have taken him to the Halifax bus depot, he felt that he must use his motorcycle to get to work on time. He was stopped at King Cross by an alert policeman, and told that he should have waited for the next bus. The magistrates agreed, fining him ten shillings, plus five shillings costs for, "Using motor fuel unlawfully."*

If a lack of petrol affected the people of Halifax and Calderdale less than, say, shortages of butter and shoes, it was still one of a series of pin-pricks that made daily life a struggle on the Home Front. With imports and domestic production concentrating on the war effort, then Chad may not have been so far from the truth if he had simply said, "Wot No Anything?" What had once been commonplace items now became almost unobtainable luxuries – crockery, kitchenware, cutlery, safety pins, shoelaces, candles, elastic, batteries and much more. Daisy Uttley, working at Hartley's in Hebden Bridge, always looked forward to the visit of the man who came around the factories as a pedlar. The tray around his neck contained nothing glamorous, just everyday items that were no longer 'everyday,' such as pins and elastic, which somehow he had obtained. He did very good business.

"spoons chained to counters at canteens and station buffets."

Shortages led to some strange consequences. Cutlery was only being manufactured at one quarter of its pre-war level, and it was not uncommon to find spoons chained to counters at canteens and station buffets. Glasses were so short that it was advisable for customers to take their own to their 'local,' only to find often enough the depressing notice on the door, 'No Beer Today.' Razor blades were difficult to find, and it was said that an old one could be kept sharp by rubbing it in warm water against the inside of a glass tumbler…if you had one!

Even matches disappeared from the shelves from time to time. Distempering became the re-decorating solution in the absence of wallpaper. People were asked to return their empty toothpaste tubes to the shops, as well as wooden cotton spools. Perhaps alarm clocks should have been classed as a 'war essential.' Those who decided that they were a luxury, resulting in a shortage, may have had servants to awaken them. For the rest of the population, it was a matter of somehow waking up so as not to be late for work and labelled 'unpatriotic.'

Both beer and spirits became short in supply due to pressure on limited quantities of sugar and grain. They became expensive too, with beer reaching a price of 1s 3d (7.5p) a pint in

1944, as opposed to a pre-war price of 6d (2.5p). Cigarettes were in desperately short supply. These have always been regarded as a necessity rather than a luxury by some, and at a time when smoking was both much more widely practised and socially acceptable, the lack of tobacco was keenly felt.

> *A packet of Virginian cigarettes became a prized acquisition as strange, new (and unpopular) brands, such as Pashas, appeared in shops. Discarded butts became ever shorter as smokers inhaled to the very last shreds of tobacco by means of holding the end of a cigarette with a pin. If even the despised Pashas were not available, the last desperate measure was to smoke tea leaves wrapped in brown paper.*

Those who took on the thankless job of shop assistant at a time when there was very little to sell, found that they received more verbal abuse over cigarettes than anything else. In spite of this danger, one Todmorden woman who did the job had her own ideas about priorities. Soldiers were stationed at Todmorden and every morning, as the shop was opened, there would be 20 or 30 seated on a low wall opposite, waiting hopefully. They could be neither classed as locals or regulars, but she made sure that the soldiers got their 'fags and baccy' first. This annoyed some civilians, but she felt amply rewarded when a captain came to thank her, and to say how much it meant to the men.

As might be expected, enormous ingenuity was shown by women to counter the shortage of wartime cosmetics. The humble and unlikely beetroot came to the rescue, the juice of which could be used as a face foundation (combined

---

"Hello Oxo legs,"

---

with calamine lotion) and a lipstick substitute, sealed with vaseline. The lack of nylons was a perennial problem, and in 1942 the government even made an appeal to women not to wear stockings in the summer. Onion skins produced a leg dye, but a more usual solution to cater for a night out was gravy browning on the legs, with eyebrow pencil carefully applied to replicate stocking seams. The 'short termism' of this approach was always demonstrated when it rained, and the kids were never fooled anyway. The streets of Halifax, as elsewhere, often resounded to the shouts of, "Hello Oxo legs," from the cheekier children.

The virtual disappearance of consumer goods that had once been taken for granted came as a shock, but perhaps not a surprise. What did come as a surprise was the disappearance of certain features of the townscape that might have been regarded as permanent. On August 7th 1940, the Halifax Town Council approved the removal of the boundary rails around People's Park and Belle Vue. The destination of the railings, along with many others to follow from the district? Salvage. This was a keynote theme in the fighting of the war on the Home Front, although it was aluminium rather than scrap-iron that was the target of the first campaign. On July 10th 1940, a joint appeal for aluminium was made by Lord Beaverbrook, Head of Aircraft Production, and Lady Reading, Head of the Women's Voluntary Service. Aluminium for aircraft was requested, and the specific target was the housewife – 'Send Your Pans Flying.'

The appeal lasted for two months, and undoubtedly the glamour of the Spitfire, and its heroic role in the Battle of Britain that was raging during those months, played a major part in the near frenzy of surrendering aluminium pans that ensued. Housewives pitched in enthusiastically, and even some one-legged veterans from World War One wanted to give up their aluminium artificial limbs. Around 1,000 tons of aluminium was collected, enough for several squadrons of fighters, but in reality there never had been a shortage of aluminium. It is likely that Beaverbrook's campaign was more of a morale boosting exercise for civilians – the creation of a feeling of national unity and purpose. It was just as well that this was not realised at the time, for

113

the desperate dearth of kitchenware throughout the rest of the war probably caused many a housewife to regret her earlier impulsiveness. In fact, one was heard to remark wistfully as an aircraft went overhead that her pans were airborne again.

Scrap metal of all types was gathered in by local councils with as much zeal as was being displayed by the housewives. The Halifax Council, and neighbouring urban and rural district councils, removed the wrought iron railings enclosing parks and public buildings. Churches, cemeteries and some private property were caught up in this railings crusade as the blow torches got to work. Out of the nearly six million tons of salvage collected in these years, five million tons was made up of scrap metal. For one reason or another much of it was never smelted down and made into steel, but was left to rust in large mounds dotted around the country. What made this all the more regrettable was the fact that many objects of historical value disappeared in the cull including, locally, two Russian 68 pounder guns captured at the siege of Sebastapol in

There was a huge and enthusiastic response to this appeal.

A sad end to the Crimean cannons in People's Park.

Courtesy of Stephen Gee

1855 during the Crimean War. They had been a proud feature of People's Park, Halifax, since 1857, but were cut up for salvage in March 1941. Too late the government realised that sometimes what was being done with the best of intentions was historic vandalism, and in August 1942, not before much damage had been done, it stated that antiquarian objects should not be classed as scrap.

Metals formed a substantial part of salvage, but by no means all of it. Lord Woolton's kitchen waste rapidly began to fill the pig bins from 1940, but the government urged the public to realise that almost everything could be recycled – paper, glass, rubber and even bones. The WVS threw itself wholeheartedly into salvage operations and organised house-to-house collections. It is likely too, that more of the materials were actually processed than was the case with metals, and by the end of 1943, for example, paper imports had been halved. In Halifax alone, salvage collected throughout the war had generated an income to the council of £55,000. Salvage drives were an opportunity for young people to become involved in the war effort, and the boy scouts were prominent in this respect. The WVS were also keen to harness the energies of the young and children who collected rose hips (a rich source of Vitamin C) could earn 3d (1.5p) per pound at salvage centres.

Out of the frying pan . . .

. . . but *not* into the fire. That must be the rule for chop bones. No bones from meat, game or poultry, no matter how small, should be burnt, because none is too tiny to be of use to the war effort. Bones make glue, lubricating oil, explosive, animal feed and fertiliser — all vital to the nation.

What do I do . . .?

I save *all* meat, game or poultry bones from the family meals and put them out for salvage in a ventilated container, such as an old saucepan — or put them in a street bone-bin if these are provided by my local authority.

I remember that bones can be kept sweet while awaiting collection by cleaning off any odd pieces of fat or gristle, and by drying them on top of the stove, in front of the fire, or in an oven still warm after cooking.

Issued by the Ministry of Information

Space presented to the Nation by the Brewers' Society

All you ever wanted to know about bones.

LIGHT RELIEF

"A good night out for a shilling."

Donald Shaw, living at Copley, was only 17 years old at the outbreak of war on September 3rd 1939. By the close of that first weekend he was viewing the future with horror. Was it the prospect of bombing or invasion that so lowered his spirits? No – it was the government's pronouncement that, "outdoor meetings of all kinds, which bring large numbers of people together," were to cease until further notice. To some this meant football matches, but to Donald it meant the end of 'monkey runs,' whereby groups of nice young men 'accidentally' bumped into groups of nice young ladies, particularly on Sunday afternoons. Donald feared that his two favourite 'monkey runs,' the one on Elland Wood Bottom, and a town centre patrol of Commercial Street, Crown Street, Southgate and Horton Street, were finished. As it happened, however, the government did not seriously interfere with the ancient courting rituals of the young males and females of the district.

The same applied to cinemas, theatres and dance halls, which by the same decree had been closed until further notice. The thinking behind it was understandable – a fear of large numbers of people being caught up in confined spaces in bombing raids. The total ban was soon lifted, and it was not just due to the almost total absence of bombing during the 'phoney' war. The government soon realised that entertainment had a powerful role to play in maintaining the morale of the people. Not only this, it provided a perfect vehicle for propaganda. Cinema in particular was at its height in terms of popular entertainment, and well fitted for this dual role. Nevertheless, public safety could not be ignored, and a red light beside the cinema screen lit up when the air raid siren sounded. An alternative form of communication was a slide which informed the audience of a warning and invited them to leave if they wished, or stay and watch the film. At first most people quietly filed out, but later the majority chose to stay and take their chance.

The popularity of cinema is reflected in the number of picture houses to be found in central Halifax and its immediate environs in 1940, 17 in all. Names such as the Odeon, the Regal, the Cinema Royal and the Electric will be quite familiar to many locals, but there were smaller and less well-known cinemas which served a loyal clientele. Whereas the Odeon housed 2,050, the aptly named Cosy had seating for a mere 698. The Alhambra and the wonderfully named Kingston Picturedrome (540 capacity) were built on similar lines.

Those who lived in the outlying districts of Halifax did not need to take a trip to town. Long vanished little cinemas, such as the Palladium at King Cross or the Pioneer at Ovenden, served their local communities, albeit with films that would be a week or two behind those on the main circuit. Alice Beaumont enjoyed a trip to Halifax for some 'main circuit' entertainment whenever she could, but found the queuing tedious. She often had to settle for her local Hebden Bridge 'fleapit,' where a seat could be booked. Another Hebden Bridger, John Tolley, found that the Picture House (a survivor even today) was often bursting at the seams. Demand was so great for a night at the 'flicks,' in spite of the perils of the blackout, that the Halifax Licensing Justices even permitted Sunday evening opening, provided that 40% of the profits went to charity.

If cinema had always been the 'theatre of dreams' for the ordinary working man and woman, an escape from drab everyday life into a world of adventure and romance, how much more so was the craving felt in wartime, when austerity was tinged additionally with anxiety? Almost anything in the romantic-escapist genre served up by Hollywood and Pinewood studios was lapped up by an eager public – 'Wuthering Heights,' 'The Wizard of Oz,' 'A Star is Born,' and that blockbuster of all blockbusters, 'Gone With the Wind.'

```
~~~~~~~~~~~~~~~~~~~~~~~~~~~~~
                THE
    Picture  House
           HEBDEN BRIDGE.
           ─────────

TO-NIGHT (Friday) at 7-15, and
TO-MORROW (Saturday) at 5-45 & 8-15:
ZORINA,
    ERICH VON STROHEIM,
    RICHARD GREENE, and
    PETER LORRE in

I Was an
        Adventuress
Alluring . . desirable . . she had known
all of life . . . and then met love!  A
picture gay . . . sparkling . . . glamor-
ously exciting . . . of adventurous in-
trigue and romance.
           ─────────
    MR. DUCK STEPS OUT.
    A Rib-tickling Donald Duck Colour
               Cartoon.
           ─────────
NEXT MONDAY, TUESDAY AND
WEDNESDAY at 7-15 each evening:

BASIL RATHBONE,
    BORIS KARLOFF,
    BARBARA O'NEIL,
    IAN HUNTER,
       VINCENT PRICE,
       NAN GREY,
And a Cast of Thousands in

Tower of London.
Built with stone and mortar . . cemented
with  blood  and  hate . . . mixed  with
women's tears!  " TOWER OF LONDON "
. . . from these  grim  walls  emerges a
terrifying drama of history's most fiendish
and fascinating characters.
~~~~~~~~~~~~~~~~~~~~~~~~~~~~~
```

A star-studded show at the Hebden Bridge Picture House in 1941, including the legendary 'Cast of Thousands.'

All the same, the opportunities for propaganda through such a popular medium were too good for the government to pass up. Films on a war theme, but with a strong story line, went down well with audiences. 'In Which We Serve,' starring Noel Coward, was one of these. Well made documentaries such as, 'Target for Tonight,' about a Wellington bomber crew, which portrayed the often quiet and calm courage of the fighting forces, made a strong impact. At the Hippodrome in Todmorden, young Vincent Holt saw a film entitled 'Western Approaches,' and was tremendously impressed by the fortitude of those often unsung heroes, merchant seamen. 'Millions Like Us' persuaded audiences to identify with others toiling away in wartime factories, all working together in one vast common purpose. 'Pathe News' could be relied upon to give an image of war with a harder edge, albeit a heavily censored one. Vincent Holt was impressed, but shocked, at the reality of seeing people killed when images of the brutal street fighting in Stalingrad first reached the cinema screen.

"American import of jitterbugging"

The live theatre, too, remained in a healthy condition during the war. The Palace and Hippodrome at Ward's End, along with the Grand Theatre and Opera House at North Bridge, provided live entertainment on a large scale. At the other end of the spectrum, with so many soldiers stationed in and around Halifax, it was decided to utilise their talents through 'Soldiers' Concerts,' offering programmes of "songs, humorous items and mouth organ solos." Public venues were given over to them, but their content was often so bawdy that they were felt not entirely suitable for young ladies to attend. Dances were popular at the Victoria and Marlborough Halls, and at the Alexandra Hall, above the YMCA, perhaps a chance to try out the American import of jitterbugging.

Wherever soldiers were billeted throughout Calderdale, mess dances were eagerly anticipated by the local girls, and another bonus was that some very good forces dance bands often provided the music. One of these, the Depolians, was formed from Royal Army Service Corps personnel stationed at Grange Mills. A young local boy who played with

Imperial Billiards Hall

SIXTEEN FIRST-CLASS TABLES.

T. HAW, Manager.

If you are in town and have 20 minutes to spare, call and have a game, Billiards or Snooker, with the popular Manager.

Improve your Snooker or Billiards by watching his play.

Ladies invited to play or watch.   **AIR RAID SHELTER.**

ARCADE ROYALE : HALIFAX

Come " INMAN " and be a " NEWMAN."   **LESSONS GIVEN.**

Billiards at the Arcade Royale offered the tempting bonus of an air raid shelter.

was 2.5d. Five 'Woodbines' set him back a further 2d, with 2d then expended on a seat in the 'Gods' at the Grand Theatre, North Bridge. The evening was completed at a fish and chip shop at Horton Street – cost 3d. Total expenditure was 9.5d, which left 2.5d for a riotous Saturday evening in Elland! Alternative diversions which Lewis could and did enjoy in Halifax were circuses on Manor Heath, snooker or billiards at the Arcade Royale, boxing at the Drill Hall and open-air wrestling at the Shay on Saturday afternoons.

If Lewis tended to patronise the Grand, then Edith Simpson was more a fan of the Palace. There was a simple reason for this. As a nurse at St Luke's – later the Halifax General Hospital – one of the few privileges she and her colleagues enjoyed was free tickets to the Palace, up in the 'Gods.' Invariably, however, the end of the

them, Ken Mackintosh, went on to become a nationally known musician. Culture with a capital 'C' was not entirely disregarded, and there was an enthusiastic response to the visit of the Halle Symphony Orchestra, under Sir John Barbirolli, to the Victoria Hall.

The almost legendary 'good night out for a shilling,' or 5p, was one that Lewis Robertshaw experienced weekly as a young man. Out of his wages as a painter, his mother allowed him one shilling spending money. Off with his mates on a Friday evening to Halifax, the return bus fare from Elland

The imposing Grand Theatre and Opera House at North Bridge – demolished by 1959.

Courtesy of Stephen Gee

performance had to be missed, for the curfew was 10 pm at the Nurses' Home. If the show was too good to leave, then it was a matter of somehow sneaking in late. Convoys of war casualties often arrived at St Luke's, and convalescents in blue flannel suits and red ties were a familiar sight. Therein lies another reason for Edith's liking for the Palace. Week in and week out, a number of 'turns' from the Palace would come up to Ward 12 - the soldiers' ward – on a Friday afternoon and give a free performance on an impromptu stage.

Light relief can often be provided by a royal visit, no matter how deep the gloom. The Princess Royal, Princess Mary, was a frequent visitor to Halifax, both in her capacity as Chief County Commissioner of the Girl Guide movement and as Commander in Chief of the British Red Cross Society. In July 1940, for example, which could fairly be described as Britain's 'darkest hour,' she brought some cheer to almost 200 officers and nurses of the Halifax detachment of the Red Cross Society by presenting certificates and awards to them. Earlier in the day, she had dropped in at the Union Street YMCA. Later visits included an inspection of ATS units at Halifax and Sowerby Bridge, and a tour of the Ovenden army convalescent camp.

Red Cross nurses often formed a detachment in the frequent parades that accompanied the big fund raising campaigns, and these too brought a spot of light relief and a dab of colour to the drabness of wartime daily life. The young took great delight in these parades, and the war brought other outlets for their energies. Boy scouts were recruited as messenger runners for ARP units, and as 'casualties' for civil defence exercises. The formation of an Air Training

'Turns' from the Palace gave free performances to convalescent soldiers.

The shaded street lamp and uniforms show that this was wartime as nurses parade down Prescott Street.

Courtesy of Stephen Gee

Corps proved so popular that two squadrons had been raised in six weeks, thus showing the continuing glamour and appeal of the RAF. The Air Defence Cadets was another variation, and a Women's Junior Air Corps was formed.

The government was very keen on this sort of thing, and at the age of 16 all boys and girls had to register with the Ministry of Labour and National Service. They were each given an interview and informed of the youth organisations through which they might do that 'bit extra' for the country, although there was no compulsion. Geoff Whiteley, of Wheatley, had his interview very late in the war and he had already joined the ATC 'Spotters Club,' based near the Three Pigeons public house in Halifax. He later became a bugler in the Sea Cadets band, and was extremely impressed at how his base – on the top floor of Crossleys at Dean Clough – had been done out as a ship.

For the millions who laboured away in factories, there was always the chance that their particular canteen would be favoured by a dinnertime visit from the 'Workers' Playtime' team. The Entertainments National Service Association, ENSA, began its life providing shows for the armed forces (who ribaldly declared that ENSA stood for 'Every Night Something Awful'), but then began to include civilian workers as well. 'Workers' Playtime' was hugely popular, and was broadcast on the radio three times a week. 'Music While You Work' could be relayed to factories the day long, and from 1944 the programme extended its reach to the armed forces. The influence of the radio as a medium for news, propaganda information and entertainment can hardly be over-estimated, for if not everyone went to the cinema or theatre, virtually everyone listened to the radio, or as it was commonly known then, the 'wireless.'

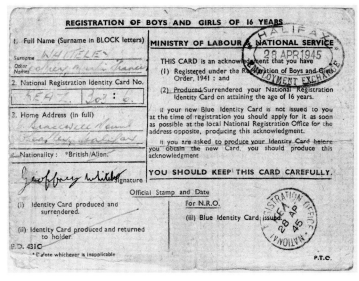

Geoff Whitely had registered to do his 'bit extra' by April 1945.

The news was, of course, heavily censored, but it was widely known that those who lived in Occupied Europe would listen to the BBC (although illegal under the Nazis) to get some approximation to the truth. War correspondents such as Richard Dimbleby, Frank Gillard and Wynford Vaughan Thomas became household names. A perhaps unnoticed innovation was that of news readers and announcers introducing themselves, so that the names of Alvar Liddell, John Snagge and Bruce Belfrage became as familiar as their voices.

There was a sound reason for the personalisation of news broadcasts. When the fear of invasion was at its height in 1940, it was felt that German saboteurs might infiltrate the BBC and put out fake 'news' broadcasts to spread panic. However, this would be much more difficult if listeners could recognise distinctive voices. In this respect, a regional accent helped, and Halifax's own Wilfred Pickles was specifically appointed with this in mind. A German impostor speaking with a Yorkshire accent would have made for some interesting listening!

Early on the in the war, the sheer novelty of 'Lord Haw-Haw' took a hold of listeners for a time. The Irish born William Joyce, working for the Germans, could command an audience of around 6 million early in 1940. There was a suspicion that the BBC news was highly 'sanitised,' and it has to be said that Joyce's playing on the social divisions in Britain sometimes struck a chord. However, if the propaganda of the BBC lay more in what it omitted, the relentless propaganda and hatred poured out by 'Lord Haw-Haw' soon palled. After the 'blitz' began, he turned from being a joke figure to one of loathing. Universally regarded as a traitor, his audience dropped dramatically in numbers.

The information aspect of the wireless was much appreciated, particularly tips from the gardening expert, Mr Middleton, or ingenious recipes on 'The Kitchen Front.' The rich and fruity tones of Dr Charles Hill, the 'Radio Doctor,' were unforgettable, and he became famous for his concentration on the bowels. In this respect, Dr Hill had great admiration for the prune, "that humble black-coated worker." To close the listening day, the equally rich Yorkshire tones of J.B. Priestley were heard, in a series entitled 'Postscripts.' These have become classics.

Perhaps more than anything, however, people listened to the radio simply to be entertained, and in this respect one show stood out 'head and shoulders' above the others – ITMA. Tommy Handley's 'It's That Man Again,' with his motley array of characters at the Ministry of Aggravation and Mysteries (evacuated to Foaming at the Mouth) must surely have been the seed ground for the Goons, and even Monty Python. Mr Fusspot was the archetypal bureaucrat, 'Funf' the resident German spy, and the catchphrases of Colonel Chinstrap – "I don't mind if I do" – and Mrs Mopp – "Can I do you now sir?" – passed into the nation's consciousness.

In more normal times, Britain's beaches would have been regarded as holiday playgrounds rather than fighting grounds, but the war dramatically altered the idea of a traditional family holiday. The package holiday

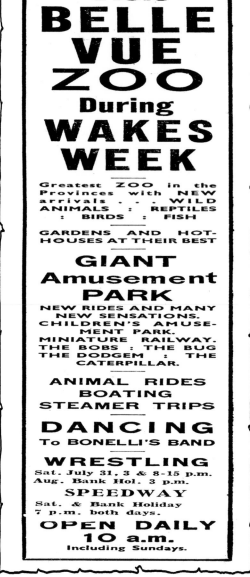

An exciting alternative to 'Holidays at Home.'

abroad for those on a limited income was a thing of the future, and people's horizons were generally confined to a week on the west or east coast of England. Even these modest ambitions were severely curtailed by the war. The government frowned on unnecessary travel, which was difficult anyway with petrol restrictions and the railways dominated by military needs. Alice Beaumont still made the effort to get from Hebden Bridge to her old haunts. She was advised that Scarborough beach was all barbed wire and tank traps, and so she gave Blackpool a go. Here she found the promenade choked with airmen being put through their marching paces by bellowing NCO's, and so she gave it up as a bad job.

For the rest of the war, along with many others, Alice had to settle for the 'Holidays at Home' option. With much encouragement from the government, each local authority organised a programme of events for the annual summer holiday week in order to provide an incentive for holiday makers to stay at home. The local 'Wakes Week' fell in August during the war years, and for Halifax it was the task of the Holiday Week Entertainments Committee to put on a feast of entertainment. Crowds flocked to Manor Heath and Shibden Park, with bulging buses disgorging thousands of eager passengers every day. The Shay, Thrum Hall and local bowling greens and cricket grounds hosted events, and money raised was often on behalf of the Red Cross or the Halifax Comforts Fund.

The 1943 programme of events for Manor Heath gave star billing to 'Robert Gandey's Roaring Jungle Express Zoo Circus.' Comedian Jim Nolan with his 'Variety Follies' came not far behind, featuring a conjuror, a dance team, a trick cyclist and a juggler. Jim himself, topping the bill as a "star comedian," jollied everyone along as a compere. As if this wasn't enough, there was a Grand Talent Competition daily, a Marionette Theatre, dog and poultry

shows, Punch and Judy, a flower and vegetable show, dancing displays and the mysterious Sam Correy with 'Spitfire Toby.' Throughout the week, the crowds were regaled with music from both the Royal Engineers Dance Band and Concert Party, and a Fire Service Band.

LUDDENDEN FOOT CO-OP HALL.

6-30. Chantry Singers with Norman Fuller (B.B.C. and Northern Concerts).

Friday, August 13th, 1943.

2-30. Paul Capser in a Programme arranged for Children.
3-45. Talent Spotting Competition, Historical and Character Costume Competition, Comic Character Competition.
4-45. Gordon Mitchell's Concert Party (Large Marquee).
4-45. Paul Capser presents His "Friends of the Children"—Punch and Judy.
6-0. Paul Capser presents Mystifying Magic for Adults.
7-0. "8 Belles" Concert Party (Marquee).
Bowls and other Competitions. Music at intervals for Dancing.

Saturday, August 14th, 1943.

2-30. Rothwell Bower in Comedy Scena arranged for Children.
3-0. Paul Capser—Punch and Judy.
3-30. Sowerby Bridge Home Guard Band.
3-30. "Merrions" Dancing Display.
3-30. Mannequin Parade and Cavalcade of Fashion (Marquee).
3-45. Demonstration of Alsatian Dogs by the Kirkstall Alsatian Training Society.
4-0. Rothwell Bower—Ventriloquial Act (Adults).
5-0. Paul Capser in specially arranged Programme for Children.
5-30. "Merrions" in Folk Dancing.
6-0. Finals—Talent Spotting, Historic and Character Costume Competition and Comic Character Competition; with Rothwell Bower.
6-30. Mannequin Parade and Cavalcade of Fashion (Marquee).
6-30. Paul Capser in "Magic for all."
6-45. Demonstration of Alsatian Dogs by the Kirkstall Alsatian Training Society.
7-0. Sowerby Bridge Home Guard Band.
8-0. Prize Distribution for various Competitions.
Music at intervals and for Dancing to 9 p.m.

Sunday, August 15th, 1943.

7-30. Musical Festival—Local Choirs and Sowerby Home Guard Band. If wet, Bolton Brow Chapel. Choir Rehearsal, Thursday August 5th, Bolton Brow Chapel.

Part of a varied programme for Luddenden Footers holidaying at home.

Courtesy of Calderdale MBC Libraries, Museums and Arts

'Holidays at Home' programmes for other years were of a similar nature, and it is noticeable that the entertainment was in a light vein, very much with the object of taking people's minds off the war. This was true throughout Calderdale, where each local council put on its own programme annually, and they provided a contrast to the great campaigns, such as 'Wings for Victory,' with their inevitably military slant. One attempt to introduce the latter (an exercise in Shibden Park in 1942 in which a Home Guard platoon destroyed an 'enemy tank' with live ammunition) had gone a little wrong when a spectator had been injured. Perhaps the message from then on was, "Keep it light."

BEATING THE 'SQUANDER BUG'

"Is the Squander Bug in your shopping bag?"

Wars cost money – in the case of World War Two a vast amount as far as Britain was concerned. She was fighting a conflict on a global scale, and such a war could not possibly be financed from taxation alone. Britain had to borrow huge amounts from the USA and persuade her own people to 'invest' in the war. The government had to wage a ceaseless campaign to promote War Bonds, Defence Bonds and National Savings Certificates and, in the process, defeat the 'Squander Bug.'

This devilish little creature, sometimes covered in a rash of swastikas, was one of the more imaginative of the government's propaganda inventions. It often could be found whispering in the ear of a lady, urging her to spend unnecessarily rather than save and contribute to the war effort. Allied to this negative image were the powerful messages, linked to duty and patriotism, urging people to invest in the government, the war, and ultimately, in victory. These sentiments permeated the early 'Feed the Guns' poster, addressed specifically to the people of Halifax. It also invoked that spirit of competition with other towns which was to play such a prominent role in the huge savings drives that were to come. It was a nice touch to link variously priced certificates and bonds to precise sizes of shell or weights of explosive, making fragile pieces of paper more immediate as tangible weapons of war. To complete the picture, the government gave a rosy glow to the sheer financial good sense of such an investment in terms of security and interest.

IS THE *SQUANDER BUG* IN YOUR SHOPPING BAG?

LOOK in your shopping bag before you start out and make sure you've left that Squander Bug behind! He's the Fuehrer of fifth-columnists—the little demon who makes you spend good money on useless things instead of recruiting it to fight for Britain. There's one certain way to squash him : put every penny you can into Savings Certificates.

Savings Certificates cost 15/- — and are worth 20/6 in 10 years —increase free of income tax. They can be bought outright, or by instalments with 6d., 2/6 or 5/- Savings Stamps through your Savings Group or Centre or any Post Office or Trustee Savings Bank. Buy now !

ISSUED BY THE NATIONAL SAVINGS COMMITTEE

The evil 'Squander Bug' – out to undermine the war effort.

For the Honour of
HALIFAX
FEED THE GUNS!

OUR Soldiers know that the greater our Gun-Power, the sooner the War will end in final Victory. They watch the WAR BOND totals. They read what each City and Town and District has sent to feed the Guns. Send a message to those lads who have gone out from your own home. Give them something to be proud of this day.

When they hear of the big total invested in National War Bonds and War Savings Certificates by their own friends and neighbours and fellow-citizens, they will realize that **your** local pride, **your** patriotism, **your** public spirit have been shown, not in words alone but in deeds. Let them see, let them feel that your whole heart is with them in the fight !

There are towns which in one short week have lent £5, £20, £50, even £75, for every man, woman and child of their population. They are watching to see what you will lend to feed the

Guns. Now is the time to show them. YOU must not be outdistanced.

In the recent fighting our Guns hurled forth more than 10,000 tons of shells every day for 15 days in succession. Mountains of shells—millions of pounds worth—are still needed to shatter the Hun defences, and to SHIELD OUR MEN as they advance. Help to provide them.

Whatever the sum at your disposal—thousands of pounds in the bank or a handful of cash in your pocket—put it all into War Bonds or Certificates. If you can afford a £5,000 Bond, buy that. It would pay for a thousand rounds of the deadly shrapnel hurled forth by our huge 60-pounder Guns.

If you can only afford one £5 Bond, or one 15/6 Certificate—buy that ! Your £5 Bond would pay for a 5 inch Shell. Your 15/6 Certificate would purchase fourteen pounds of High Explosive.

Feed the Guns with
WAR BONDS
and help to end the War.
You will get the BEST and SAFEST of all Investments.

The money you lend to-day will bring you such a return as investors before the War never dreamed of getting on gilt-edged Government Securities backed, as War Bonds and Saving Certificates are, by all the wealth and power of the British Nation.

Your country will give you 10/- interest yearly for every £10 you invest in War Bonds, and will add to the value of your War Savings Certificates every year, until you get £1 for every 15/6 you invest. You can sell your Bonds or cash your Certificates at any time (with the interest due) if you need the money.

An appeal to duty and patriotism – not forgetting economic good sense.

Courtesy of Calderdale MBC Libraries, Museums and Arts

The impetus to save, of course, was undoubtedly helped by rationing and the general scarcity of things to buy. Nevertheless, it was an impressive statistic that by June 1943 almost one quarter of the population belonged to one of the country's 300,000 savings groups. Schools and workplaces were the ideal places to promote war savings. Pupils were issued with National Savings booklets and school was pitted against school in weekly savings competitions. Jean Fields was attending Pellon Lane Board School when it triumphed in one of the competitions, and her sister was photographed for the local newspaper as the proud representative of the winning school. There may have been less of the voluntary spirit in the factories, where both Harold Doyle at Asquith's and Stanley Newton at Waller Bros of West Vale, found money compulsorily deducted from their wage packets to buy War Bonds. The vouchers received instead were to be cashed in after the war as Post-War Credits.

Even before the drives to persuade people to lend money to the government, there were more urgent matters that required the citizens of Britain simply to give money. In the Summer of 1940, with Hitler on the shores of France and the Low Countries, there was no doubt in the minds of the British people that all that stood between this country and an invasion was a handful of fighter aircraft and their gallant pilots. Lord Beaverbrook, Minister of Aircraft Production at the time, made an urgent appeal, both for the aluminium to build more planes, and the cash to pay for them. Local housewives enthusiastically answered the request to 'Send Your Pans Flying,' and Halifax was one of the first towns to enter into serious fund raising. With its graceful lines and its fighting prowess, the Spitfire captured the public's imagination, and so it was a Spitfire Fund that was established in Halifax on September 1st 1940. Elland followed suit the next month. The chief organiser for the Halifax campaign was Sir Harold Mackintosh, and an eye-catching programme of events was put on. This ranged from the standard fare of jumble sales, bridge parties, and concerts at the Grand Theatre and Odeon Cinema, to more novel ideas, such as a competition to guess how far a 10 hp Vauxhall

The Mayor of Halifax, Alderman Barker, runs an auction in aid of the war effort.

Courtesy of Stephen Gee

car would travel on a quart of petrol. The highlight must surely have been the flight of Hurricanes performing aerobatics over Halifax. Both Philip Hanson and Geoff Whiteley, schoolboys at the time, bought little wooden Spitfires for their lapels, whilst Jean Fields took every opportunity to visit the Town Hall where a giant mock thermometer kept a record of how the fund was climbing week by week. By October 7th 1940 the Halifax Spitfire Fund had reached over £12,000 and it closed at the end of the month at just short of £13,000, enough to pay for two Spitfires. Halifax firms contributed one tenth of the total, and the rest was due to the generosity of the townspeople. The Halifax effort 'made waves' nationally, and Sir Harold Mackintosh's organising ability led him to being later appointed as Chairman of the National Savings Committee, thus leading the nation's war savings drives.

"a fly-past of Spitfires over Elland"

Elland was keen not to be outdone by Halifax, and it too put on a colourful programme of events, capped by a fly-past of Spitfires over Elland. The great 'coup,' however, was the bringing of a captured Messerschmitt 109 to Elland. Fondly labelled 'Mrs Smith,' it was put on display in the Town Hall Square. Having only begun its fund in October, the Elland Spitfire drive concluded in November 1940, having raised a total of just over £6,600. This was enough to pay for a Spitfire, and for many years a plaque from Lord Beaverbrook hung in the council offices in Elland. It recorded an achievement which had "earned the gratitude of the British nations." The efforts of other local districts should not be forgotten. Sowerby Bridge, for example, had raised just over £2,100 when it declared its Spitfire Fund closed in December 1940.

The three Spitfires funded by Halifax and Elland came off the production line at Castle Bromwich,

in Birmingham, in March 1941. They carried the serial numbers P8092 ('Elland'), P8903 ('Halifax I') and P8095 ('Halifax II'). 'Elland' did duty as a training plane for young pilots, as well as front line duties, prior to its retirement in September 1944. 'Halifax I' may have been involved in action against German attackers over Coventry, Nottingham and London. In May 1942 it was transferred to an officer training unit, but only two months later it was involved in a flying accident and was 'written off.' 'Halifax II' played a part in attacking enemy airfields in France in 1941, and also did escort duty for British bombers, before being allocated to air service training in July 1941. 'Halifax II' remained in this role until it was withdrawn from service in April 1944.

The local Spitfire Funds were just a taste of things to come as the government launched huge annual drives across the country, each one with a different focus. The towns and cities of Britain chose the week during which they would throw their weight behind a particular campaign. Hardly had the dust settled after the closing of the Spitfire Fund than 'War Weapons Week' was upon the people of Halifax. It was stressed in the official programme of events that the aim was not to seek gifts and donations of money, but loans in the shape of purchase of government bonds and certificates. The target was not modest - £1,000,000 in a week for Halifax alone – a staggering sum!

You may be interested to know the approximate cost of some of the War Weapons :	
	£
Battleship	8,000,000
Cruiser	2,000,000
Destroyers	from 320/450,000
Submarine	350,000
Bomber Aircraft	20,000
Medium Tank	15,000
Anti-Aircraft Gun	from 3/6,000
Fighter Aircraft	5,000
Torpedo	2,000
Barrage Balloon	700
Light Ambulance	300
Machine Gun	100
Rifle	7
1,000 rounds of Ammunition ...	£5 10s.
Hand Grenade	4s.
Bullet	6d.

HERE IS AN AIM FOR EVERYONE.

OUR OBJECT FOR HALIFAX is at least £1,000,000 and if possible to SET A NEW RECORD—for Yorkshire at least—PER HEAD OF POPULATION

Let us brace ourselves for this task, so that those precious things which are the heritage of free men and women will endure.

A shopping list of military hardware for Halifax.
Courtesy of Calderdale MBC Libraries, Museums and Arts

Halifax 'War Weapons Week' was officially opened by Lady Snowden, who launched a Schools' Poster Competition on Friday, December 6th 1940. The week really began to get into its stride the following day, with a ceremonial parade through the centre of town by the Duke of Wellington's Regiment and on this first day the sum of £350,000 was raised. As the week progressed, the red column on the giant thermometer outside the Town Hall continued to rise steadily as the public flocked to see exhibitions of weapons, demonstrations of weapons training and bomb disposals, a war photographs display, band performances, physical training to music and yet more parades.

By Saturday, 14th December, the official ending of Halifax 'War Weapons Week,' all expectations had been exceeded. Bonds and certificates to the tune of just over £2,500,000 had been sold. This represented £26 10 s per person when the average weekly wage for a skilled worker stood at around £5. A national record was created and the Chancellor of the Exchequer declared that, "You should indeed be proud of having set up such a standard of patriotism to the rest of the country."

It is difficult to comprehend how a sum of around £2,500,000 can have been raised by ordinary working people, and it has to be assumed that the per head average must have been boosted by some pretty hefty contributions from the more wealthy citizens and commercial enterprises of Halifax. The national record, however, did not last long, and even locally only two months. At this time, the town of Elland seems to have operated on the principle that anything Halifax could do, Elland could do at least as well, if not better. It ran its 'War Weapons Week' in February 1941, and set to with such vigour that on 25th February, to great rejoicing in Town Hall Square, it was announced that Elland had raised just over £650,000. This worked out at the astounding sum of £33 15s 5d per head of population,

Elland's near neighbour, Brighouse, was also doing its bit – 'War Weapons Week' 1941.

Courtesy of Stephen Gee

beating Halifax handsomely. Some attempt was made to work out the contributions of 'small investors' and, remarkably, this came out at just over £7 per head. Councillor John Wilson, chairman of the Elland fund raising committee, invited Sir Harold Mackintosh to visit Elland, accompanied by a giant-size tin of toffees. This was, in fact, what Sir Harold was wanting to promote – keen inter-town rivalry.

Elland's achievement became the 'benchmark' for other local drives. A splendid effort was made by Hebden Royd in its 'War Weapons Week' of March 1941, when the per head total almost touched £30, and in April and May Sowerby Bridge and Brighouse were not far behind with per head totals of £29 8s 6d and £27 0s 7d respectively. Just to keep the ball rolling, in September 1941, as part of the national 'Speed the Tank' campaign, Halifax enjoyed a three day visit from two Valentines and one Matilda tank, plus two 20 ton

LEND TO WIN

Hebden Royd and Hepton is asked to lend £150,000 during the coming War Weapons Week — sufficient to provide Five Motor Torpedo Boats .... Can we do it?

YES! — and more than that, if we all play our part. Let every Man, Woman and Child, and every Firm and Institution in the district rally to the call by investing in the World's Safest Security.

Full details from your Savings Group, Hon. Official Agents, Investment Centres, Banks, the Post Office, or from Hebden Royd & Hepton War Weapons Week Committee, or Secretary, at the Education Offices, Pitt Street, Hebden Bridge.

During War Weapons Week buy:—

  3% SAVINGS BONDS
  2½% NATIONAL WAR BONDS
  3% DEFENCE BONDS
  SAVINGS CERTIFICATES
           and increase your deposits in the
  POST OFFICE SAVINGS BANK.

Remember! You will NOT be asked to give, but to LEND. These Government "Gilt-edged" Interest bearing securities are the best investment you can possibly make.

HEBDEN ROYD & HEPTON WAR WEAPONS WEEK
MARCH 15-22

A specific aim for Hebden Royd and Hepton – five motor torpedo boats.

conveyors and an armoured scout car. They were on view at Savile Park and Bull Green, helping to forge that vital link between those who were making the weapons and those who were using them.

Fund raising was not confined to government or local council initiatives. The Halifax YMCA, for example, accumulated an impressive £15,000 in its 'war chest' in a drive of September 1941. The little red triangle of the YMCA was a familiar and welcome sign for all servicemen in a strange town or city. YMCA centres provided baths, refreshments and recreational facilities. Hebden Royd raised £3,000 to provide a YMCA hut at a Yorkshire Bomber Station, which was dedicated in October 1941.

Other massive local annual campaigns followed, although none quite matched up to the achievement of 'War Weapons Week' - £5,334,931. The navy was the theme of 1942, and each town and city held its 'Warship Week.' No better focus of attention could have been found, with the Royal Navy locked in a deadly battle with the U-boats in the North Atlantic. Their attacks on merchant ship convoys bringing food and other vital supplies

Thrilled crowds on the streets of Halifax witness the 'Speed the Tank' campaign of 1941.

Courtesy of Stephen Gee

were threatening to defeat Britain by starvation. As an inland town with a regimental barracks, Halifax had no special link with the navy, but everyone could appreciate the crucial role it was playing. Also the campaign gave the opportunity for towns to 'adopt' ships and engender goodwill links of potentially great value. Thus 'Ajax for Halifax' was the theme of the town's 'Warship Week,' which ran from February 7th to 14th 1942.

Halifax adopted the prestigious cruiser, 'Ajax,' for its 'Warship Week' of 1942.

Courtesy of Calderdale MBC Libraries, Museums and Arts

'HMS Ajax' was a notable ship, a cruiser which had played a prominent part in the Battle of the River Plate, in December 1939, the result of which had been the scuttling of the German pocket battleship, 'Graf Spee,' in Montevideo harbour. Halifax's 'Warship Week' was opened at the Town Hall by the Rt Hon A.V. Alexander, First Lord of the Admiralty, on February 7th 1942. A week of parades and concerts followed, but the novelty and excitement of the link with

the navy was enhanced by recreating the bow of the 'Ajax' in Bull Green. Hence the Home Guard band could play music from the 'Quarter Deck,' whilst daily running totals were announced from the 'Bridge,' at noon, by various civic dignitaries. The target was £1,500,000. Local Sea Cadets must have been thrilled at the opportunity of manning the Bull Green 'Ajax!' Accompanying the various events, there were exhibitions of war photographs in the Drill Hall, Prescott Street, along with models of both the 'Ajax' and the 'Ark Royal.'

The result of Halifax 'Warship Week' was finally announced from the 'Bridge' by the Mayor D.W. Smith Esq, at noon on

Powerful publicity in the battle for cash.

Wednesday, February 18th 1942. The nautical expression that had been used throughout the week – 'the signal is to save' – had been well observed and the huge sum of £2,077,565 12s 3d had been spent on war and defence bonds, the total being proudly displayed on the flagpole of the replica. The per head total of £21 17s 9d broke the previously held national record held by Liverpool, and upheld the reputation for generosity of the citizens of Halifax. The 'goodwill' aspect was considered to be important, and in August 1942, officers and men from the ship visited Halifax and there was an exchange of plaques.

"Elland's adopted ship was the destroyer, 'HMS Eclipse,'"

Unsurprisingly, by this time Halifax's national record had long been broken, and equally unsurprisingly, Elland had been the culprit. Elland's adopted ship was the destroyer, 'HMS Eclipse,' and on March 4th 1942 the town's per head total for its 'Warship Week' was announced as being just over £25. Other local townships all completed their naval weeks by the end of March. Ripponden had adopted the corvette, 'HMS Convolvulus,' on North Atlantic convoy duties. A party of Ripponden officials and fund raising officials visited the ship, and it seems as if the £80,487 raised was totally for the ship itself.

Queensbury and Shelf had adopted 'HMS Vervain,' and Hebden Royd 'HMS Bradford.' Sowerby Bridge took a slightly different line and its chosen vessel was the submarine, 'HMS Unsparing.' Everyone listened with special interest for news of the exploits of their adopted vessels and the people of Todmorden must have been delighted in 1943 to hear that 'their' ship, the destroyer 'Vidette,' had sunk a U-boat in the Atlantic with depth charges. Adoptions, however, did not protect ships from the vagaries of war. Todmorden's pride in 1943 must have been matched by Queensbury and Shelf's sadness in March 1945 when the 'Vervain' was sunk - this at the last gasp of the European war.

Plaque from Halifax's cruiser, 'Ajax.'
Courtesy of Calderdale MBC Libraries, Museums and Arts

Plaque from Elland's destroyer, 'Eclipse.'
Courtesy of Calderdale MBC Libraries, Museums and Arts

There was a lull before the next major campaign, but just to ensure that the 'Squander Bug' did not rear its ugly head in the meantime, a 'Tanks for Attack' campaign was launched later in 1942, but on a rather more low-key note. Interestingly, however, this drive marked a change in emphasis from defence to attack. The tide of war was turning, and the change was even more apparent in the 1943 major effort – 'Wings for Victory.' Heavy bombing of Germany was now underway, but aircraft losses were high and enormous amounts of money were needed both to replace aircraft and manufacture huge quantities of bombs. 'Wings for Victory' publicity stressed the importance of knocking out Germany's industrial capacity as a route to victory, but retaliation for the 'blitz' was often touched on by speakers at public meetings.

It was a source of pride to Halifax people that one of the main bombers of the day carried the town's name, which was bestowed on it by Viscountess Halifax in a ceremony at Radlett in September 1941. It would be nice to think that this was in recognition of Halifax's renowned efforts in financing the building of two Spitfires in 1940, but the explanation is a little more mundane. Handley

HALIFAX HITS Where it Hurts.

Back that punch with a power that will knock the Nazis out for good. Every penny you lend is effective to prove your pride in the fine achievements of Halifax Bombers; and to back their efforts and speed victory.

£1,500,000
for
36 "HALIFAXES"

is the target we are out to hit. Let's crash in with all the savings we can muster and realise another record for Halifax.

INVEST NOW IN

3% Defence Bonds
3% Savings Bonds
2½% National War Bonds
Savings Certificates or in the Post Office Savings Bank.

HALIFAX WINGS for VICTORY WEEK

MAY 22-29

'Wings For Victory' 1943 and the emotive link between Halifax and Halifax.

Page had a custom of beginning the names of their aircraft with either an 'H' or an 'S,' and Halifax was perhaps chosen as embodying the spirit of hard-work and determination.

It was Ripponden, however, which set the pace locally, and its 'Wings for Victory' week, between May 15th and May 22nd 1943, raised £175,334. The per head total of around £35 briefly gave it the Yorkshire Championship Flag, until Halifax pinched it a week later with an incredible total of just over £3,334,000 at a per head average of £36 12s. The opening speeches of the Ripponden week give some clue as to how such tremendous sums of money could have been raised when mention was made of a £10,000 contribution from the Halifax Building Society. Ripponden's efforts were probably boosted by the presence at the opening ceremony of a distinguished visitor, Air Vice-Marshall Norman Bottomley. Born in Ripponden, the son of a cotton spinner, he had been commissioned into the Royal Flying Corps in 1916. By 1943 he had risen to be Deputy Chief of Air Staff at Bomber Command, and in 1945 was to replace Arthur 'Bomber' Harris as its Chief.

"At last it was the turn of the 'poor bloody infantry,'"

At last it was the turn of the 'poor bloody infantry,' and 1944 saw 'Salute the Soldier' as its major campaign. By this time British soldiers, supported by their tanks and artillery, had slogged their way across North Africa and up Italy, had engaged the Japanese in the Far East and were poised, along with their allies, to attack occupied France. A huge effort would be needed to dislodge the Germans, and so 'the soldier' became the focus of 1944 fund-raising. Elland kicked off the local efforts in May 1944, but perhaps inspired by the success of 'D'-Day, June 6th 1944, Brighouse turned in a really good performance. Its 'Salute the Soldier' week of June 3rd to June 10th raised £370,877.

In his opening address in Thornton Square, Brighouse, the chairman of the Savings Committee, Brigadier R.E. Sugden, was able to

quote a letter from an old comrade. Field Marshall Montgomery no less, had offered his encouragement to the Brighouse campaign. The week's offerings of parades, concerts and

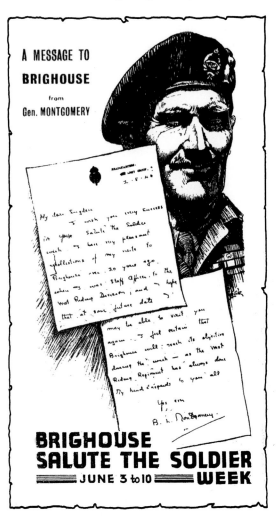

Did Brighouse have friends in high places in 1944?

exhibitions was enlivened by an anti-aircraft gun display by the Royal Artillery at Wellholme Park, and a cricket match between Brighouse Town Council and the Rotary Club. One very novel element was a display of Army cooking on show in a shop at Hutchison Buildings, Commercial Street, prepared by the Army Catering Corps. The local newspaper described it as, "a mouth-watering display of eatables" – a little at variance with the usual comments of the 'foot-sloggers' about their daily fare! The Royal Engineers proved very innovative in their contribution to Brighouse 'Salute the Soldier' week. Having built a raft on the river, they charged 2d for a return trip from the old fairground to Lillands Farm. All passengers were given a photograph of another old soldier – Winston Churchill.

At the end of the war, in 1945, there was a 'Thanksgiving Savings' effort in Halifax and Calderdale. This raised a relatively small amount as compared to some of the mammoth totals of the previous years. People may now have been suffering from 'savings fatigue,' or perhaps every available tin, jug and jar was so stuffed with government bonds and certificates

A Physical Training display in Elland as part of its 'Salute the Soldier' effort in 1944.

Courtesy of Stephen Gee

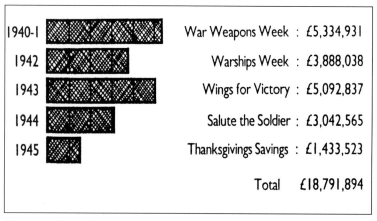

1940-1		War Weapons Week :	£5,334,931
1942		Warships Week :	£3,888,038
1943		Wings for Victory :	£5,092,837
1944		Salute the Soldier :	£3,042,565
1945		Thanksgivings Savings :	£1,433,523
		Total	£18,791,894

The magnificent financial effort made by Halifax and Calderdale.

that they felt the time had now come to give the 'Squander Bug' a chance. Nationally, the sum raised by all the great savings campaigns was, roughly, £2,777 million – truly a tribute to the willingness of the British people to get behind the war effort. Halifax and Calderdale won a well-earned reputation for generosity, the expression of this being a magnificent total of £18,791,894.

PICKING UP THE THREADS

"We may allow ourselves a brief period of rejoicing."
Winston Churchill, May 8th 1945.

Very early on the morning of May 8th 1945, a Halifax lady was on her way to work. She was very tired and her mood was in no way improved by the sound of singing in the streets. Voices shouted a brief message to her and she suddenly shed her tiredness like a skin – the war was over! Hitler's suicide in his bunker amidst the ruins of Berlin, one week earlier, had speeded up the process of Germany's collapse. Italy had already gone out of the war and on May 7th 1945 the European war ended with the unconditional surrender of Germany. A two-day public holiday was declared in Britain, beginning with 'Victory in Europe Day,' May 8th 1945.

At last, after almost six long years of toil and hardship, the struggle in Europe was over and the time had come for celebration. Long disused flags and bunting were dug out of storage and street parties took place from one end of Calderdale to the other. Somehow or other, in spite of rationing, party food was conjured up for children as tables and chairs were dragged outside. Churchill broadcast to the nation at 3 pm and people needed no second invitation to participate in what he described as, "a brief period of rejoicing." They knew what he meant – the war with Japan was not yet over – but for the moment it was time to 'let their hair down.' The streets in the centre of Halifax became thronged with celebrating crowds and there was open-air dancing in Bull Green and Southgate. Festivities intensified with the arrival of evening, and as floodlights illuminated Wainhouse Tower, Bull Green House and the Odeon Cinema, street dancing continued well into the night.

Over in Hebden Bridge, young John Tolley managed to resist all warnings and mounted the roof of Redman's Factory to 'help' his father and fellow workers mount a large Union Jack. Only about half a mile away, young Keith Newbitt was not so lucky. He had just gone down with, of all things, 'German' measles, and had to miss all the festivities. It was no consolation to hear Dr Dowdall suggest that he might call them 'Empire' measles. As 'VE Day' became 'VE Night,' the street lamps came on, in itself still a novelty, for blackout regulations had only been totally lifted on

Peace breaks out at Priestley Place, Beechwood, Sowerby on May 8th 1945.

Courtesy of Stephen Gee

135

A struggling mass of revellers celebrates 'Victory in Europe Day' on Southgate, Halifax.

Courtesy of Stephen Gee

24th April. The night was further illuminated by the twinkle of bonfires throughout the area. There was not much wood to spare, but enough combustibles had been scraped together to make this night a miniature 5th November, with Hitler doubling up as Guy Fawkes.

Vincent Holt and his pals managed to build a bonfire on the steep Lumbutts hillside at Todmorden. They decided to make it a night to remember by taking up blankets, tents and a drop of illicit cider. As the night wore on, however, and the fire burned low, Vincent became aware of a more reflective mood stealing over the group. Adolescents they may have been, but they were recognising that there was more to this moment in history than simply wild celebrations, and they retired to their tents with spirits rather subdued – in spite of the cider. In fact, there had been a more sober undercurrent to the festivities throughout the day. The large crowds who had gathered outside Halifax Town Hall to hear an address by the Mayor, Alderman L. Chambers, had been reminded that victory had only been achieved through the supreme sacrifice of many men and women – "those who have given all that we might have this freedom."

There were households throughout the district for which 'VE Day' was nothing more than a sad reminder of loss, households to which men would not return or where the fate of their menfolk was unknown. Then again, there were Halifax and Calderdale men still engaged in the continuing war with Japan, or held in appalling conditions in Japanese prison camps.

Dora Longbottom, of Copley, spent a quiet 'VE Day' as she thought of her husband, from whom she had heard nothing for about three and a half years. A driver in the Royal Artillery, Willy Longbottom had embarked from Scotland in December 1941, bound for Singapore. Having been captured in Java, Willy was moved to Japan, where he had to endure working up to his knees in water in coal mines.

The dropping of atomic bombs on Hiroshima, on 6th August 1945, and on Nagasaki on 9th August, led to the ending of the fanatical resistance of the Japanese. The real end of the war could now be celebrated with 'Victory over Japan Day,' August 15th 1945. Then, and only then, did Dora Longbottom receive a tiny note from her husband to say that he was all right. Shortly afterwards she received back all the letters she had sent to him – undelivered and unopened.

"in temperatures of up to 120 degrees in the shade."

Suffering and death had been the fate of many who had fallen into the hands of the Japanese. At least Willy Longbottom did return, albeit down to a weight of seven stone from a previous fourteen stone. A drastic loss of weight was a common characteristic of all the returnees, including Lance-Bombardier William Turner, the first former Japanese prisoner to return to Hebden Bridge. He had been working in Siam (Thailand) in temperatures of up to 120 degrees in the shade. Weight could be restored, but for some men who came back with diseases such as malaria, their health was broken forever.

And so Halifax and its surrounding area had 'seen it through.' In theory there had been no need to fight at all. Britain could have done a deal with Hitler in 1939 or 1940. Local people, however, were at one with the rest of the nation in recognising the untrustworthiness of the dictator. They perceived, perhaps better than some of Britain's leaders, that agreements were worthless with a man whose ambitions seemed limitless. They regarded Hitler as a bully; would not submit to tyranny; and fought to preserve freedom and their democratic way of life. Slow to arouse, the British people with their Imperial allies then fought with a stubbornness and determination which surprised everyone but themselves.

Shortly after 'VE Day,' when films of the liberation of Belsen and Buchenwald were shown to horrified cinema audiences, people could see that their suspicions as to the true nature of Hitler's régime had been correct, and that this had indeed been a 'just war.'

Gains such as the preservation of democracy and freedom were important, if rather intangible. The costs were more tangible. Eleven local citizens were killed, and ten injured, in the Hanson Lane bomb incident of November 1940. Calderdale and Halifax servicemen (and one woman) were killed or injured in almost all the land, sea and air engagements in which Britain was involved. One of these gained the highest possible award for gallantry, the Victoria Cross. Sergeant Hanson Victor Turner, a former bus conductor from Copley serving in the West Yorkshire regiment, was in command of a platoon which found itself in great danger in Burma on June 6th 1944. He made five grenade attacks on the Japanese lines before being killed on the sixth. He was posthumously decorated with the Victoria Cross.

The VC won by Sergeant Hanson Victor Turner in Burma.

Courtesy of Calderdale MBC Libraries, Museums and Arts

Each war death was a tragedy, but some were tinged with the kind of cruel irony that wars always produce. One local member of a Lancaster aircrew survived for three days on a raft in the Atlantic when his plane was shot down. He later survived a Lancaster crash-landing in Scotland, only to die, aged 20, whilst training recruits in the seemingly secure environment of Oxfordshire. Two of the training aircraft collided in mid-air. Local seamen died in most of the major naval actions but, sadly, more lost their lives on the Japanese transport, 'Lisbon Maru,' than on any other single ship. This vessel was carrying British prisoners-of-war from Singapore as Allied armies advanced towards the city, and it was sunk by Allied action.

The war produced casualties in many senses. Whilst most men returned to their homes and families and slipped back into civilian life relatively easily, it was not the same for all. Some men, although physically unharmed, were so mentally scarred by their experiences that they were never quite the same men again. Others found that long years of absence had irreparably fractured their former family relationships and that 'picking up the threads' was impossible. Husbands away and wives at home had sometimes formed bonds that were stronger than the old ones and marriages disintegrated.

> *Virtually all families where the absence of a husband or father had been a long one felt some sort of strain. Children suddenly found themselves confronted by a stranger who expected to be obeyed. A wife who had carried all the responsibility for family decisions for several years might bridle at a husband who decided that he wanted military style discipline in the household.*

At the other end of the spectrum, some couples found that a long parting had only strengthened their mutual bonds and that they now appreciated each other so much the more. The ebb and flow of military personnel, and the waves of evacuees, had created a new network of relationships across the country – sometimes disruptive, often beneficial.

And what of the people we met at the beginning of this story, reacting in their different ways to Neville Chamberlain's fateful broadcast on that warm and balmy Sunday morning of September 3rd 1939? At Claremount, Marjorie Talbot's distress at the

---

"to live in a hole in the ground for three days."

---

prospect of her boyfriend being sent abroad was in no way eased by subsequent events. Jim Brennan, a regular soldier in the Black Watch, was dispatched to France. Fighting in a rearguard action, he was captured at St Valery in June 1940. He ended up in prisoner-of-war camps in Poland and Danzig. Here he was very glad of the food parcels that came from Marjorie, the Red Cross and the USA, even though the ill-fed German guards always took their share. Jim, believing that it was every soldier's duty to try and escape, attempted to smuggle himself out of Danzig in the hold of a ship bound for Sweden. Having been betrayed, his punishment was to live in a hole in the ground for three days. 'VE Day' fell on Marjorie's birthday, 8th May, and it was a day of absolute delight for her. In August 1945, Marjorie Talbot and Jim Brennan were married – a union that was to last until Jim's death, 56 years later.

All's well that ends well – the marriage of Marjorie Talbot and Jim Brennan in August 1945.

That first Sunday of the war had found Mary Prout in a somewhat different mood to the one that Marjorie Talbot was experiencing. Holidaying in the Isle of Man, Mary had hoped that the war would trap her there, so prolonging her holiday indefinitely. This was not to be. Returning to Halifax, she married, became Mary Crossley, and soon had a baby to care for. She saw the war out in Halifax, the most memorable moments for her being the arrival of the Dunkirk evacuees and the bomb which fell uncomfortably close to where her baby was sleeping at her mother's house in Hanson Lane.

Stanley Topliss, the ten year old in Hebden Bridge who was filling cans with water on the first day of the war, soon came to realise that Hitler's incendiary bombs would take a little more than this to stop them. A few years later he was doing war work as an apprentice engineer in Sowerby Bridge, had joined the Air Training Corps and was an avid collector of militaria. For Lewis Robertshaw, in Elland, the

Petty Officer John Wall – a long and painful separation.

opening of the war had coincided with his putting a coin in the cap of a tramp who was playing a fiddle outside his home. Lewis went on to join the Home Guard and then the Yorkshire and Lancashire Regiment. He embarked overseas as a married man and was not to see his newly born daughter again until his next leave, about three and a half years later. As was the case with so many soldiers, his daughter recognised him only from photographs.

As for John and Nellie Wall, of Spring Hall Lane, the ominous words uttered by Neville Chamberlain on September 3rd 1939, had only deepened the anxiety they felt about their 6 year old daughter, June. She was not expected to live beyond the age of 15 because of the hole in her heart, and if John Wall was conscripted, there would be even fewer years for him to spend with his daughter. John eventually did receive his 'call up' papers – in August 1942 – and joined the Royal Navy, leaving behind his pregnant wife and sick daughter. Much of his time was spent in Canada and in April 1943 his second daughter, Patricia, was born. He never saw her for the first three years but, perhaps worse, he never saw June in those years either. Sadly, the doctors' prognosis was exactly right, and June died in January 1948, shortly after her fifteenth birthday. The concept of 'sacrifice' took many forms during the war.

June Wall with young sister, Patricia. June had very few years left to her.

Whatever the shape or form of the sacrifice, the time had now come, with the end of the war, for people to feel that it had all been worthwhile. Above all, people were looking for a better life than had been offered to many in the 1930s. It is in this light that one of the most astonishing election results of the twentieth century must be seen. Labour won an overwhelming victory in July 1945, emerging with an absolute majority of 146 over the other parties combined. The British people rejected their great wartime leader, Winston Churchill, in favour of Clement Atlee and his promise to create a Welfare State in which people would be protected, "from the cradle to the grave." Foreign observers were stunned, as was Churchill himself, but he would have been the first to admit that this was what the war had been all about – the freedom of people to choose their leaders. Churchill himself visited Halifax and the Calder Valley on June 4th 1945, making stirring speeches to large crowds. In spite of this, local voters followed the national trend, and Labour candidates took the Halifax, Sowerby and Elland seats comfortably from their sitting Conservative opponents.

Labour's 'brave new world' was not going to be easy to achieve. No country had fought in the war longer than Britain and her Empire. The cost had been stupendous, bringing Britain to the brink of financial ruin, and not helped by the fact that the USA abruptly cut off all financial aid after August 17th 1945. The government's attempts to provide new housing, a National Health Service, a new education system, and better insurance and pensions schemes, were set to a background of grim post-war austerity. Rationing continued (not to end totally until 1954) and even worsened briefly when, for the first time, bread went on ration. The early months of 1947 produced one of the worst winters on record, accompanied by fuel and power crises.

People wondered if the war had actually ended as the grim struggles of life continued. Had 'seeing it through' all been worthwhile? It would be. Everyone just had to hang on a little longer. Starting with the morale boosters of the Festival of Britain in 1951 and the Coronation of 1953, the "never had it so good years" were on their way. Better times were coming – just around the corner.

Churchill in Halifax prior to an astonishing election result in 1945.

Courtesy of Stephen Gee

BIBLIOGRAPHY

GENERAL BOOKS

Asa Briggs: 'Go to It' - Working for Victory on the Home Front 1939-45; Mitchell Beazley, 2000.

M. Brown & C. Harris: The Wartime House – Home Life in Wartime Britain 1939-45; Sutton, 2001.

R.A. Freeman: Britain at War; Arms and Armour Press, 1990.

N. Longmate: How We Lived Then; Pimlico, 2002.

S.P. Mackenzie: The Home Guard; Oxford University Press, 1995.

Readers' Digest Association Ltd: Yesterday's Britain, 1998.

A.J.P. Taylor: English History 1914-1945; Pelican, 1973.

A.Valery: Talking About the War 1939-1945; Michael Joseph,1991.

LOCAL BOOKS/PUBLICATIONS

Calderdale at War: Bankfield Museum, 1982.

Defence of Britain Project 1995-2000: local information gathered by T.R. Hornshaw & F.Roper.

Down Memory Lane: R.Hardcastle & E.Riley, 1981.

Evening Courier Millennium Souvenir 1900-1999: compiled by Val Watts.

Halifax Courier and Guardian Historical Almanacks, 1938-1946.

It Were No Laughing Matter: Calderdale Voices 1930-1945; edited by L. McGillivrey & J. Thornton; Yorkshire Arts Circus, 1987.

Memory Lane – Recollections of Todmorden (1988), Sowerby Bridge (1990) and Brighouse, Rastrick and Hipperholme (1992): these three compiled and edited by staff of Calderdale Libraries.

Nothing Interesting Ever Happened To Me: Calderdale Voices – Illingworth and Mixenden Communities, Yorkshire Arts Circus, 1987.

Ryburn Valley Reflections: compiled and edited by J.Mallinson-Akroyd, 1991.

Transactions of the Halifax Antiquarian Society (New Series) as follows:-
Local History from World War II : the 'Starfish' sitesat Cragg Vale & Clifton,
by Donald Haigh MA, FSA
(Volume I, 1993).

'Starfish' Decoys and Targets in Calderdale & West Yorkshire,
by Donald Haigh MA, FSA
(Volume XII, 2004).

Calderdale and the Wars of the Twentieth Century 1899-1945,
by T.R. Hornshaw (Volume VI, 1998).

NEWSPAPERS

The Halifax Daily Courier and Guardian

The Hebden Bridge Times

The Todmorden News and Advertiser

The Brighouse and Elland Echo

INTERNET

Lancashire Aircraft Investigation Team: www.lait.ukonline.co.uk

LIST OF CONTRIBUTORS

Thanks to the following who provided help, information and/or photographs.

Donald Akroyd

Geoff Allinson

Joan Baldwin

Marjorie Brennan (Talbot)

Marjorie Brierley

Iain Cameron

Rosalind Connolly

Kathleen Crabtree

Mary Crossley (Prout)

Vera Cuttle (Blenkinsop)

Raymond Dean

Harold Doyle

Mary Doyle

Alan Duckworth

Harry Fielden

Pauline Fielden

Brenda Gaukroger (Goldthorpe)

Dennis Greenwood

Philip Hanson

Chris Helme

Jacqui Hirst

Ken Hirst

Vincent Holt

Jeane Holmes (Edwards)

Joan Hopwood

Norman Hopwood

Pat Hubbard (Wall)

Verena Hurren

Kathleen Iredale

Trevor Jackson

Colin Jagger

Tom Lawlor

Harry Leah

Dora Longbottom

Bertha MacDonald (Pottinger)

Diana Monahan

Keith Newbitt

Kathleen Newton (Heys)

Jennifer Pell

Stan Pierce

Ray Riches

Lewis Robertshaw

Fay Robinson

Doreen Russell

Edith Scotford (Simpson)

Donald Shaw

Ronnie Shepherd

Joan Stansfield

Phyllis Stead

Peter Sugden

Max Sunderland

'K.G.' Sutcliffe

Margaret Sweeting (Brennan)

Alexander Thomas

Eric Thomas

Louise K Thomas

Luke Thomas

Lynne Thornton

Joan Titley (Sutcliffe)

John Tolley

Stanley Topliss

Harry Turner

Daisy Uttley

Colin Wakefield

Jean Wakefield (Fields)

Pauline White (Geier)

Geoff Whiteley

Hazel Whiteley (Cartwright)

Margaret Wilson (Hitchen)

Nick Wotherspoon